Lecture Notes in Computer Science 14068

Founding Editors

Gerhard Goos
Juris Hartmanis

Editorial Board Members

The series Lecture Notes in Computer Science (LNCS), including its subseries Lecture Notes in Artificial Intelligence (LNAI) and Lecture Notes in Bioinformatics (LNBI), has established itself as a medium for the publication of new developments in computer science and information technology research, teaching, and education.

LNCS enjoys close cooperation with the computer science R & D community, the series counts many renowned academics among its volume editors and paper authors, and collaborates with prestigious societies. Its mission is to serve this international community by providing an invaluable service, mainly focused on the publication of conference and workshop proceedings and postproceedings. LNCS commenced publication in 1973.

Bertrand Kerautret · Miguel Colom ·
Adrien Krähenbühl · Daniel Lopresti ·
Pascal Monasse · Benjamin Perret
Editors

Reproducible Research in Pattern Recognition

Fourth International Workshop, RRPR 2022
Montreal, Canada, August 21, 2022
Revised Selected Papers

Springer

Editors
Bertrand Kerautret [ID]
Lumière University Lyon 2
Bron, France

Adrien Krähenbühl [ID]
University of Stasbourg
Illkirch Cedex, France

Pascal Monasse [ID]
Ecole des Ponts Paris Tech
Marne- la- Vallée Cedex 2, France

Miguel Colom [ID]
Ecole Normale Superieure Paris
Gif-sur-Yvette, France

Daniel Lopresti [ID]
Lehigh University
Bethlehem, PA, USA

Benjamin Perret [ID]
ESIEE Paris
Université Gustave Eiffel
Noisy le Grand Cedex, France

ISSN 0302-9743   ISSN 1611-3349 (electronic)
Lecture Notes in Computer Science
ISBN 978-3-031-40772-7   ISBN 978-3-031-40773-4 (eBook)
https://doi.org/10.1007/978-3-031-40773-4

This Springer imprint is published by the registered company Springer Nature Switzerland AG
The registered company address is: Gewerbestrasse 11, 6330 Cham, Switzerland

Preface

The fourth edition of the IAPR-endorsed Workshop on Reproducible Research in Pattern Recognition was held in Montreal on August 21, 2022, as a satellite workshop at ICPR. Following the three previous editions, this event covered advances on reproducibility platforms, on new reproducible research results, and on ICPR companion short papers. Taking advantage of the end of the pandemic, the workshop was able to propose a full in-person event, with just a few remote presentations.

As in previous editions, four ICPR companion papers were accepted for oral presentation and the program was completed with a total of seven presentations, including talks focused on concepts or experience feedback of reproducibility. 81% were authors who had never published at RRPR before. This rate is quite stable with respect to the two previous editions (85% and 89%). To address the absence of contributions for the Reproducible Research framework, a new "Lightweight" presentation type was proposed. This mode facilitates author participation by submitting a single abstract first and then allowing authors with more time to prepare their contribution to the post proceedings. Each submitted paper was single-blind review by three to four reviewers and by two reviewers for the lightweight presentation-based papers. The audience averaged 20 attendees, including authors presenting online.

For this edition, the event was extended beyond the workshop in two ways. First, RRPR continued after the in-person ICPR conference with a new open poster presentation track at the second edition of the IAPR international conference Discrete Geometry and Mathematical Morphology (DGMM), which was held two months after RRPR in Strasbourg on 24–27 Oct 2022. Two new contributions were accepted for this event and are included in the proceedings. The topic of these papers is related to the DGMM scope with a special focus on reproducibility. This new initiative was a further step towards improving awareness of the RRPR events and also towards cross-fertilizing the topic of "reproducible research" across a wide range of IAPR activities, since it applies everywhere. In fact, this was the initial goal of embedding the RRPR workshop within ICPR. Additionally, we were pleased to extend the workshop interaction beyond the workshop itself by including two focus groups initiated during the event. The first group discussed the efforts to integrate reproducible research in international conferences and the second one was oriented to motivate reproducible research and to measure the balance between impact versus investment. These discussion groups were extended for six months after the workshop and the resulting discussion report was compiled into a paper reviewed by an editorial board member. In the end, 9 papers were reviewed and 5 full papers were accepted after revision, thanks to the post-proceedings process, and 4 short companion papers were also accepted.

The proceedings contents were organized into three main categories. The first axis is on the reproducible research framework with one paper resulting from the lightweight presentation mode focused on efforts for reproducible research, updating a platform survey published in the second edition of RRPR. A second category, on reproducible research results, includes one paper dealing with the extraction of document information using graph neural networks. A third group includes ICPR companion papers describing implementation and details that are absolute requirements for reproducibility. Several topics are addressed by these papers such as continual learning, log clustering, anomaly detection and video classification with multispectral imaging. The fourth group results from the new special reproducibility track of the DGMM event and includes a paper focusing on segmentation from CNN combined with max-tree methods and another contribution on forest road extraction. Finally, the last part of the proceedings includes the discussion report mentioned above.

Finally, as usual, we would like to thank all researchers who submitted contributions to RRPR and also the reviewers of the scientific committee. We also address a special thank to the IAPR organizers, who gave their support once again to RRPR with the official endorsement of IAPR. The edition of these post-proceedings was also made easier by the *EasyChair* platform and the responsiveness of the editorial team at Springer-Nature. Finally, we also warmly thank again Audrey Bichet from the MMI department of the IUT of Saint-Dié-des-Vosges who made the nice poster for this fourth RRPR edition.

June 2023

Bertrand Kerautret
Miguel Colom
Adrien Krähenbühl
Daniel Lopresti
Pascal Monasse
Benjamin Perret

Organization

Chairs

Miguel Colom	Centre Borelli, ENS Paris-Saclay, France
Bertrand Kerautret	LIRIS, Université de Lyon 2, France
Daniel Lopresti	Lehigh University, USA
Pascal Monasse	École des Ponts ParisTech, France
Jean-Michel Morel	Centre Borelli, ENS Paris-Saclay, France
Benjamin Perret	Université Gustave Eiffel, France
Hugues Talbot	CentraleSupélec, France
Burak Yildiz	Delft University of Technology, Delft, The Netherlands

Special Track on Geometry and Deep Learning Chairs

Carlos Crispim-Junior	Université de Lyon 2, France
Nicolas Mellado	IRIT, CNRS, Université Paul Sabatier, France
Jonathan Weber	Université de Haute-Alsace, France

Reproducible Label Chair

Adrien Krähenbühl	University of Strasbourg, France

Program Committee

Fabien Baldacci	Université de Bordeaux, France
Jenny Benois-Pineau	Université de Bordeaux, France
Partha Bhowmick	IIT Kharagpur, India
Arindam Biswas	IIEST Shibpur, India
Alexandre Boulch	Valeo.ai, France
Luc Brun	Ensicaen, France
Leszek J. Chmielewski	Warsaw University of Life Sciences, Poland
David Coeurjolly	CNRS, Lyon, France
Miguel Colom	Centre Borelli, ENS Paris-Saclay, France
Carlos Crispim-Junior	Université de Lyon 2, France

Isabelle Debled-Rennesson	LORIA, Université de Lorraine, France
Pascal Desbarats	Université de Bordeaux, France
Maxime Devanne	Université de Haute-Alsace, France
Éléonore Dufresne	University of Strasbourg, France
Véronique Eglin	INSA Lyon, France
Philippe Even	LORIA, Université de Lorraine, France
Yukiko Kenmochi	Laboratoire d'informatique Gaspard-Monge, CNRS, France
Bertrand Kerautret	Université de Lyon 2, France
Pierre Kraemer	University of Strasbourg, France
Adrien Krähenbühl	University of Strasbourg, France
Jacques-Olivier	Lachaud Université Savoie Mont Blanc, France
Daniel Lopresti	Lehigh University, USA
Vincent Mazet	University of Strasbourg, France
Enric Meinhardt	Centre Borelli, ENS Paris-Saclay, France
Nicolas Mellado	IRIT, CNRS, Université Paul Sabatier, France
Cyril Meyer	University of Strasbourg, France
Serge Miguet	Université de Lyon 2, France
Pascal Monasse	École des Ponts ParisTech, France
Nelson Monzón	López Universidad de las Palmas de Gran Canaria, Spain
Jean-Michel Morel	Centre Borelli, ENS Paris-Saclay, France
Pierre Moulon	Meta, USA
Khadija Musayeva	Université Côte d'Azur, France
Phuc Ngo	LORIA, Université de Lorraine, France
Nicolas Passat	Université de Reims Champagne-Ardenne, France
Benjamin Perret	Université Gustave Eiffel, France
Thanh Phuong	Nguyen University of Toulon, France
Fabien Pierre	LORIA, Université de Lorraine, France
François Rousseau	IMT Atlantique, France
Loïc Simon	Ensicaen, France
Isabelle Sivignon	GIPSA-lab, – CNRS, France
Robin Strand	Uppsala University, Sweden
Hugues Talbot	CentraleSupélec, France
Iuliia Tkachenko	Université de Lyon 2, France
Laure Tougne	Université de Lyon 2, France
Antoine Vacavant	Institut Pascal, Université Clermont Auvergne, France
Jonathan Weber	Université de Haute-Alsace, France
Laurent Wendling	LIPADE, Université Paris Cité, France
Burak Yildiz	Delft University of Technology, Delft, The Netherlands

The Fuzzy Boundaries of Reproducibility (Lightweight Presentation Abstract)

Daniel Lopresti[1] and George Nagy[2]

[1] Lehigh University, Bethlehem, PA, 18015 USA
lopresti@cse.lehigh.edu
[2] Rensselaer Polytechnic Institute, Troy, NY, 12180 USA
nagy@ecse.rpi.edu

Abstract. Issues that arise in applying current reproducibility practices to pattern recognition include contradictory definitions of "reproducibility" versus "replicability," the missing connections between these notions and the arguably more useful concept of "generalizability," the distinction between assessing an experiment and assessing the evaluation of an experiment, and the lack of a formal framing that would allow us to agree with mathematical certainty that a particular result is indeed reproducible / replicable / generalizable.

In this short talk designed to prompt debate, we will draw from a few recent papers that advance the notion of reproducibility. The challenges go well beyond what can be accomplished by simply sharing source code. We will then sketch some alternatives for relating generalizability to reproducibility, experiments that could be instructive as we advance in this direction, and suggestions for how we might start to formalize such notions so that we can write with precision and confidence about them in the future.

Keywords: Reproducibility · Pattern recognition · Performance evaluation · Research communities.

Contents

Discussions Report Paper

Reproducible Research Framework

Development Efforts for Reproducible Research: Platform, Library and Editorial Investment

Miguel Colom[1] , José Armando Hernández[1] , Bertrand Kerautret[2(✉)] ,
and Benjamin Perret[3]

[1] Université Paris-Saclay, ENS Paris-Saclay, CNRS, Centre Borelli,
91190 Gif-sur-Yvette, France
miguel.colom-barco@ens-paris-saclay.fr
[2] Univ Lyon, Univ Lyon 2, CNRS, INSA Lyon, UCBL, LIRIS, UMR5205,
F-69676, Bron, France
bertrand.kerautret@univ-lyon2.fr
[3] LIGM, Univ Gustave Eiffel, CNRS, ESIEE Paris, 77454 Marne-la-Vallee, France
benjamin.perret@esiee.fr

Abstract. Reproducible research in pattern recognition can be viewed from a number of angles, including code execution, platforms that promote reproducibility, code sharing, or the release of libraries providing access to relevant algorithms in the corresponding disciplines. In this work, after recalling the motivation and classic definitions of reproducible research, we propose an updated overview of the main platforms that might be used for reproducible research. We then review the different libraries that are commonly used by the pattern recognition, computer vision, imaging and geometry processing communities, and we share our experience of developing a research library. In the third part, new advanced editorial investments will be presented, such as the IPOL journal or other IPOL-inspired new initiatives like OVD-SaaS.

1 Introduction

In general, research publications first highlight new theoretical or methodological advances related to scientific problems, while reproducibility is rather considered as a secondary point. While these academic distinctions and measures seem natural from an innovation perspective, the emphasis on reproducibility should also be a key point in avoiding the credibility crisis denounced by Donoho [1]. Reproducibility also has an impact on long-term research, such as simplifying comparisons to make research results more meaningful.

The Fig. 1 shows the evolution of the ratio of publications mentioning the words "Reproducible" or "Reproducibility" in general and engineering topics

This research was made possible by support from the French National Research Agency, in the framework of the projects WoodSeer, ANR-19-CE10-011, ULTRA-LEARN, ANR-20-CE23-0019, and by the SESAME's OVD-SaaS project from Région Île de France and BPI France, and Ministry of Science, Technology and Innovation of Colombia (Minciencias), call 885 of 2020.

B. Kerautret et al. (Eds.): RRPR 2022, LNCS 14068, pp. 3–21, 2023.
https://doi.org/10.1007/978-3-031-40773-4_1

(graphics (a) and (b) respectively). During the last 30 years, the mention of the reproducible research (RR) topic remains almost constant in the general domains while it steadily increased in the engineering domain. This increasing interest is also visible through the development of platforms for reproducible research [2]. For instance, since the publication date of this latter review, new major platform appeared like the *ReproducedPapers.org* platform [3] that allows researchers to share reproduction experience on papers especially in the machine learning field. Such a new platform reaches also educational purpose with, for instance, the integration of reproducibility into fairness, accountability, confidentiality and transparency in artificial intelligence [4]. Another example of new advance is the development of the *ReproServer* [5] that follows the previous ReproZip tools [6]. ReproServer is an open source web application allowing to reproduce experiments from a web browser and based on the ReproZip tool. The REusable ANAlyses system called REANA [7] is also another example started after the review on reproducible research platform [2]. This initiatives answer to the need of the reuse, re-validation, and re-interpretation of research works.

The platform evolution is not the only point that contributes to RR, since the development of libraries is also a meaningful ingredient if we consider the algorithm implementation point of view. It also contributes to the diffusion of scientific contents and also simplify code review in a editorial process where not only the classical paper is reviewed but also the associated source code. To put these efforts in perspective with reproducible research, the following section reviews new platforms that have been recently proposed. Then, the investment in libraries will be detailed by several examples taken from the pattern recognition domain and the experience of creating a new library will be shared by the Higra library creator (Sect. 3). Finally, in Sect. 4, the investment on advanced editorial initiative will be detailed with the recent progress around IPOL journal and a related new service oriented project OVDSaaS useful for the deployment of reproducible industrial applications.

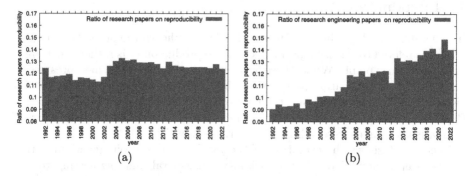

Fig. 1. Evolution of the Reproducible Research ratio of publications from the general (a) and engineering (b) topics. The data were extracted from ScienceDirect (https://www.sciencedirect.com) database on August 29, 2022.

2   Reproducible Research Platform Updates

In the previous work [2], we have classified the major reproducible research platforms into three broad categories. The first group is the online execution platforms. It includes platforms like *RunMyCode*, *CodeOcean* or *Jupyter*, all of which allow to directly run code on a distant web server. The other group called dissemination platforms, is more focused on hosting source code archive package with a referencing system. In this category, we can mention *RunMyCode* which also proposes to host source code, *DataHub* or *ResearchCompendia*. The last category is the peer-reviewed journals, composed of three main journals: *IPOL*, *ReScience* and *Insight Tool Kit*.

Proof of the growing interest in reproducible research, new platforms have appeared since the previous publication and several of them such as *DagsHub*, *Paper with code*, *Replicate* or *Hugging Face Spaces* are now referenced from *arXiv* open access platforms.

ReproducedPapers.org [3]   *- Dissemination Platforms -*

This platform was introduced in the context of machine learning reproducibility and teaching activities at a master level degree. The main ideas of the platform  are the following. First, a researcher suggests on the platform a paper to be reproduced. Then, from the proposed paper, different types of contributions can be submitted: (i) a replication including re-implementation from scratch, (ii) a reproduction where existing code is evaluated, (iii) hyper-parameters check including sensitivity of parameters, (iv) new data to test the result on other contexts, (v) new algorithm variant, (vi) new code variant including improved implementation, (vii) ablation study. A resulting pdf paper or web page describing the new contribution is then made freely available to the community, including source code (for (i) and (vi)) or new data (for (iv)). When the submission is proposed, a review is conducted to ensure that the main contributions match those that have been announced.

Figure 2 presents the evolution of the number of papers proposed for reproduction as well as the number of reproduction published since the platform was created. Both the research papers proposed for reproduction and the reproduction attempts are increasing. In average, there are around two reproductions per proposed article. This trend looks positive for the future of the platform.

Replicability.graphics [8]   *- Dissemination Platforms -*

The aim of this platform focused on computer graphics is to evaluate the replicability of the papers published at the SIGGRAPH conference. The evaluation is presented in the form of a light review describing the difficulty of the reproduction. This evaluation can result from the direct code execution, when available, or from the re-implementation of the article. The ease of re-implementation is usually evaluated by the platform reviewers who have a strong experience in the computer graphics domain. In total, 454 papers were reviewed on the platform, covering SIGGRAPH events from 2014 to 2021, with 192 papers proposing code and 146 papers were evaluated as replicable. The remaining papers (25% with 116 papers) were evaluated difficult to replicate.

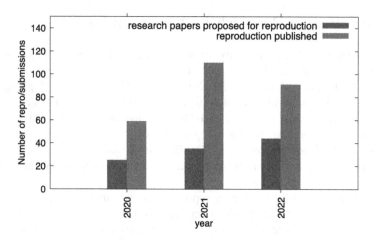

Fig. 2. Evolution of the activity of the https://reproducedPapers.org platform.

PapersWithCode [9]   *- Dissemination Platforms -*
Introduced by *Meta* in 2018, this platform references papers associated with
source code theoretically enabling the replication of the paper. It can be considered as a dissemination platform since only the paper and the source code
are referenced. The platform can be useful to researchers interested to reuse the
related proposed methods. However, unlike the previous two platforms, no details
are provided on the potential difficulty of reproduction or conformity between
source code and algorithms. With a total of more than 126 000 papers[1], it covers
various domains with different portals like Machine Learning (76.2%), Computer
Science (8.8%), Physics (6,0%), Astronomy (3.3%), Mathematics (3.3%), Statistics (2.4%). Papers can also be associated with datasets, methods and evaluation
tables. Users can submit a paper and its implementation from a free user account.

Dagshub.com   *- Dissemination Platforms -*
This platform is specialized in the machine learning domain with an experience comparable to *GitHub* but integrating specialized tools for the visualization of models and machine learning pipelines. It allows users to manage experiments,retrieve the best data or parameters, and is therefore useful for optimizing
results and sharing experiences with other users. It contributes to facilitate the
reproducibility, in particular with an easy configuration of automation pipelines
running on *GitHub actions* or other web-hooks. The platform is free for public
and limited private repositories and chargeable for more intensive use with private cloud or enterprise access. In 2023, the platform was used by 23,000 data
scientists and 400 organizations. The Fig. 3 shows the evolution of user registration (graphic (a)) and update activities over the last four years with the focus
on repositories, datasets or models (graphic (b)). These measures highlight the

---

[1] Data extracted from https://portal.paperswithcode.com on 15 May 2023.

rapid success of the platform which is experiencing positive growth and are a promising sign of future user uptake.

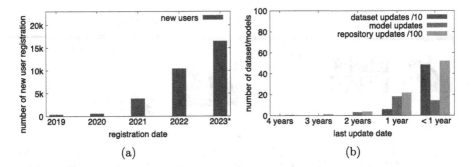

(a)   (b)

Fig. 3. Evolution of user registration (a) and update activities (b) of the dagshub.com platform. The graphic (b) displays update over time of datasets, models, or repositories. The data were obtained from the page listing the different ressources from the dagshub.com explore page. *For the 2023 year year, the number of user registrations was interpolated by taking the double of registrations of the 6 first months of 2023.

HuggingFace.co **- *Online Dissemination & Execution Platforms* -**
Originally launched in 2016 as a company developing a chat bot application for teenagers, the Hugging Face Hub can now be seen as straddling the line between dissemination and online execution platforms. Based on a *git* repository whose main structure is comparable to that of *GitHub*, it focuses on models and datasets, with a section called *Space* containing a playground allowing users to run the model directly online. The platform integrates various models with custom configurations and weights fine tuned on specific training sets. The dissemination part is advertised as forever free while the computational ressources is limited according to the subscription chosen by the user (free for two basic CPUs and chargeable for more advanced GPUs).

Reana [7]   **- *Online Execution Platforms* -**
Oriented toward reproducible research and data analysis, this platform is designed to create workflows by using external sources (like *GitHub*, *GitLab*). This platform can play a main role in reproducible research, however it is actually reserved to CERN (European Organization for Nuclear Research) users which limits its potential impact.

ReproZip [5]   **- *Online Execution Platforms* -**
At the origin *ReproZip* was first an open source tool designed to bundle all the necessary contents to reproduce research results. Then a *ReproServer* was associated to *ReproZip* enabling to extract and run the resulting program. Actually as mentioned by the authors the full construction of the platform is in progress. The main idea of such a platform appears promising for the future. Unlike the previous *Reana* platform, the current project is more oriented towards open

access and unrestricted use which could be an important factor for its future growth.

       (a)   (b)   (c)

Fig. 4. Illustration of the Replicate.com: (a) overview, (b) parameter setting before online execution and (c) link appearing from the *arXiv* platform highlighted in red.

Replicate.com   *- Online Execution Platforms -*
The main motivation of this platform is to apply machine learning to real world problem without complex code installation. It can be considered as mainly a machine learning code replication platform. User can construct and upload their package allowing the reproduction of their research results based on their own machine learning models. The platform proposes three ways to reproduce results: by using a direct online execution process, by running a platform API or by running the code directly on the user computer. The Fig. 4 illustrates this platform from the front page (image (a)), the main page allowing to set the parameters of a particular demonstration (image (b)) and the *arXiv* referencing this platform (image (c)). Unfortunately this platform is not free (users can try it for free with a limited processor time allocation).

The Table 1 shows the recent platform comparison using the criteria defined in [2]. In order to complete the comparison context, the result of the platform best covering the different criteria is reported on the last line of the table with the IPOL platform. This platform still leads the ranking with eight validated criteria and is now followed by *Reproduced Papers* and *Replicate.com*, which satisfied seven criteria.

3   Reproducible Research Through Libraries

In addition to RR platforms, efforts to contribute to reproducible research are also visible through the development of libraries offering implementations of algorithms and tools. To give an overview of the library development types, we first review different initiatives in the discrete geometry and mathematical morphology community before detailing an example of an author initiative with the development of the Higra library (Hierarchical Graph Analysis) which could help new researchers to understand and anticipate the important steps to create, publish and maintain a new library.

Table 1. Recent platform comparisons using the eleven criteria introduced in previous work [2].

Platform	(1)	(2)	(3)	(4)	(5)	(6)	(7)	(8)	(9)	(10)	(11)
Reproduced Papers	✓	✓	✓	✓	✓	✓	✗	✗	✓	✗	–
Replicability.graphics	✓	✓	✓	✗	✓	✗	✗	✗	–	✗	–
Papers With Code	✓	✓	✓	✗	✓	✓	✗	✗	–	✗	–
Dagshub.com	(A)	✓	✓	✗	✓	✗	✓	✓	✗	✗	–
HuggingFace.co	(A*)	✓	✓	✗	✓	✗	✓	✓	✗	✓	–
reana	✗	✗	✓	–	✗	✓	✓	✓	–	✗	–
ReproZip	–	–	✓	–	✓	✓	–	–	–	✗	–
Replicate.com	(A*)	✓	✓	✗	✓	✓	✓	✓	✗	✓	✗
IPOL	(B)	(C)	✓	✓	✓	✓	✓	✓	✓	✓	✗

Criteria:

(1) Free to use

(2) No mandatory registration

(3) Several programming languages allowed

(4) Peer-reviewed code and data

(5) Easy to use by the non-expert

(6) General scope

(7) Possibility to upload user data

(8) Interaction through a web interface

(9) Access to a public and persistent archive of experiments

(10) Design of automatic demonstration from textual description or visual tool

(11) Allow to modify the source code before execution

Legend:

– Not Applicable.

(A) Partially free (paid for non entreprise or restricted private projects).

(A*) Limited time free demonstration or basic CPU (then paid by time usage of CPU/GPU usage).

(B) True for demonstrations using a sample learning dataset. To use the plat- form as a service, the user needs to be connected with a role authorizing this usage.

(C) The demonstrations are free to use up to some limits (say, size of the data or computation time), but industrial use of demonstrations and applications requires payment.

3.1 Library Experiences from Pattern Recognition, Image and Geometry Domains

The Table 2 lists some of the major libraries in the domains of pattern recognition, image and geometry processing. A first group gathers libraries initiated and financed by private companies. The ITK medical imaging library, created and still managed by Kitware, is an example. On another popular topic of computer vision, the OpenCV library presents a mean of 60 contributing authors by year. As for the PCL library, the private company Willow Garage supports the development. As mentioned in our previous work, insides the development of the ITK library the *Insight Journal* aims to contribute to reproducible research by publishing algorithm descriptions together with its implementation.

Another group of libraries is composed of academic initiatives, including also the open source community. The older referenced in Table 2 is the CGal library created with the help of European project funding. The economic model was then supported by the commercialization of the research results obtained through the company GeometryFactory thus ensuring the continuation of the development of the library while contributing to the promotion of academic research. Initiated from individual initiative, the libraries CImg (David Tschumperlé, GREYC), Geogram (Bruno Levy, LORIA), Olena (Thierry Geraud, LRDE), Tulip (David Auber, LaBRI) and Vigra (Ullrich Koethe, HCI) were also contributing in helping the diffusion and reproduction of research results. Like other libraries such as OpenMVG, TTK or Higra, the DGtal library was also created from a French initiative gathering five laboratories.

Table 2. Example of librairies related to the pattern recognition, image and geometry domains. The three first libraries are mainly supported from private company including open-source community (highlighted in gray inside horizontal lines and light gray above the dashed horizontal line for mixt of private/academic).

Library	ref	domain	langage	version	#auth.	date	funding
OpenCV	[10]	Comp. Vision	C++	4.5.5	1,383	1999	Willow Garage
ITK	[11]	Image Processing	C++/Pyt.	5.2.1	265	2000	Kitware
PCL	[12]	Point clouds	C++	1.12.1	464	2010	Willow Garage
CGal	[13]	Geometry proc.	C++	5.4	123	1996	Acad./GeometryFactory
CImg	[14]	Image processing	C++	3.1.2	72	1999	Acad.
Geogram	[15]	Geometric algorith.	C++	1.7.8	7	1998	Acad./INRIA/ERC
Olena	[16]	Image processing	C++/Pyt.	2.1	50	2001	Acad. / Project
Tulip	[17]	huge graph visualiz	C++/Pyt.	5.6.2	9	2001	Acad./private
Vigra	[18]	Comp. Vision	C++	1.11	50	2008	Acad.
DGtal	[19]	Digital geometry	C++/Pyt.	1.2	27	2011	Acad. / Project
OpenMVG	[20]	Mult. View Geom.	C++	2.0	86	2013	Acad./Mikros/Foxel
TTK	[21]	Topology ToolKit	C++	1.0	36	2017	Acad. / Project
Higra	[22]	Graph analysis	C++/Pyt.	0.6.5	4	2018	Acad. / Project

If we measure the development of certain libraries over time, we can easily highlight the libraries that have been supported by or associated with private companies, as shown by the CGal library with a continuous investment during 25 years (Fig. 5(a)). On the contrary, the OpenMVG library shows a slowdown since the moment the library started to be based on the open source development mode only (Fig. 5(b)). The impact of the development of such a library on the research world can be measured by citations in research publications or the number of research projects that rely on the library. Graph (c) in Fig. 5 shows one such example measured on the Geogram library. The number of research papers referencing the library appears to be stable over time, while the number of project mentioning is increasing over the years.

This rapid overview shows that outside the benefit for reproducibility, the library development has impact on sharing results both on research publications and projects. In order to give the main steps of library development, we show an experience feedback on the main steps of the Higra library.

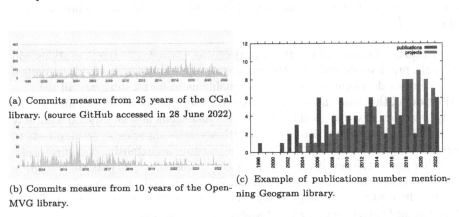

(a) Commits measure from 25 years of the CGal library. (source GitHub accessed in 28 June 2022)

(b) Commits measure from 10 years of the Open-MVG library.

(c) Example of publications number mentioning Geogram library.

Fig. 5. Example of developer investissement from two libraries (a,b) and evolution of publications and project exploiting the Geogram library (c).

3.2   Higra Library Development Feedback

Higra – Hierarchical Graph Analysis – is a C++/Python library for efficient sparse graph analysis with a special focus on hierarchical methods: construction of hierarchical representations (agglomerative clustering, mathematical morphology hierarchies, etc.), the analysis and processing of such representations (filtering, clustering, characterization, etc.), and their assessment. The development of Higra started in 2018 and is still a quite young project of moderate size. It is now extensively used for research and teaching purpose in our laboratory and is also used by researchers and practitioners in several other places in the world. The purpose of this section is to explain the different steps of this project in order to help researchers interested in creating their own libraries to enhance and facilitate the reproducibility of their work.

Deciding and Starting the Project

Project Prequel. Before starting the Higra project, our researches on hierarchical graph processing were essentially supported by two mostly internal libraries: 1) a pure C library called SM (*Saliency Map*) which was fast but lacked flexibility; and 2) a pure Python library called HiPy (*Hierachies in Python*) which was flexible but slow. Although both libraries are available online, neither was really designed for distribution to an external audience: there was mostly no documentation, no tests, and, in a general way, no project management. This approach also started to be detrimental for the research activity of our own group: at some point, we had about a dozen of forked versions of the SM library on our computation server, developed by various researchers of our team, without any documentation on the modifications made. In practical terms, this resulted in lost changes, wasted effort, and overall reduced reusability and reproducibility of our work.

Motivations. The aim of the Higra project was to overcome the limitations and solve the problems described in the previous section. The idea was to have a unified place for our developments that would enable us to better integrate all the contributions of the team and to attract external users and developers. This goal can only be achieved with a good level of project management which includes notably using a source version control system with a versioning scheme, writing tests to ensure correctness and non regression, and writing an extensive documentation. Another goal of the new library was to be easy to install and to naturally integrate into the rich Python ecosystem for machine learning and computer vision, which essentially meant supporting Numpy arrays [23] and the ability to be installed by the standard package-management system for python *pip*.

All these would enable us to achieve a more efficient use of our resources, a better dissemination of our contributions, and ease the reproducibility of our research.

Getting Started. The start of such project can be intimidating and requires some planning as several choices have to be made regarding 1) the project organization (code and documentation hosting, build-system, CI/CD pipelines) and 2) the technical development aspects (languages, external dependencies, software architecture). Many researchers are not familiar with all these aspects that are not part of their main area of expertise. Fortunately, today, we can rely on the many tools developed by the open source community and the many examples available online to make wise choices and implement them. We recommend to not neglect this initial planning and configuration phase, even if it takes a little time, because it will save a lot more time in the following phases of the project and help to deliver features quickly.

In the following, we describe the most important choices made for the library Higra and the motivations behind them. Of course, there are no absolute best choices and, in the end, this depends on many factors such as the objective of the projects and the developer preferences.

Technical Choices of the Library Structures

Languages, Architecture and Dependencies. We opted for a relatively classical organization for a data analysis project in Python with a front-end, comprising essentially high-level functions, written in Python and a core, with data-structures and critical algorithms, written in C++. We decided that the C++ core should also be usable without Python which would allow us to use these functions in another context, for example to build web demos using Emscripten[2] which allows compiling C/C++ code to javascript. This is quite different from many Python packages such as Numpy, Scikit-learn or Scipy whose back-ends rely heavily on the C-Python API. One other possibility would have been to write a pure Python package with Numba [24] which can perform just in time compilation of a subset of the Python language to improve the execution time. Numba manages to obtain excellent performances, but it complicates debugging and was, at the time we started the project, quite an experimental project.

The bridge between C++ and Python is made thanks to the Pybind11 library [25] which is a header only C++ library which enables to easily create Python module from C++ and export C++ functions in this module. Pybind11 is a very popular library used in many large projects. In order to integrate with Numpy arrays we chose to rely on the XTensor[3] C++ header only library which aims at providing a C++ substitution of Numpy with a seamless integration with Numpy arrays (C++ tensors can be converted seamlessly into Numpy arrays and conversely).

Build Tools, Unit Testing. The main build system of the project is CMake which is frequently used for C++ projects. It is available on most systems and can be installed through many package managers, including *pip* (even if it is not a Python package). Such tools become nearly mandatory when one wants to compile cross-platform projects in a reliable and reproducible way: they help to deal with platform specific options and with dependency management. We have never heard about a pleasant build system and CMake is no exception, but it gets the job done and as it is used in many projects it is easy to find examples covering many use cases. A secondary build system, *setuptools*, is used to generate Python wheels (python packages which can be installed with *pip*). This consists of a single Python script which is merely a wrapper around the CMake project.

The unit tests are written in C++ using the library Catch2[4] and in Python with the standard *unittest* package. Using a library such as Catch2 for unit tests provides many benefit such as easy test generations for template functions and types, easy logging, selective test execution and debugging, and are supported by advanced IDEs (execute/debug specific tests directly from the GUI).

Hosting and CI/CD Pipelines. We naturally opted for *Git* as source version control which is very well adapted for open source development and decided to

---

[2] https://emscripten.org/.

[3] https://github.com/xtensor-stack/xtensor.

[4] https://github.com/catchorg/Catch2.

use *Github* for hosting. The documentation is hosted by *Read the Docs*[5] which is commonly used by python packages but can also be used with C++. Python wheels are hosted by PyPi[6] which is the standard python package repository used by *pip*.

Continuous integration (CI) pipelines are managed by Github. The idea is that any pull request made on the repository first goes through automated testing on multiple platforms before being merged into the main branch. Our CI pipelines cover several versions of Python and 3 platforms: Linux, MacOS, and Windows. Each pipeline validates that the project can be built and that unit tests pass in a fresh new environment. Setting the CI pipelines is quite difficult at first if the user is not familiar with them, but it is really worth it by drastically reducing the risk of regressions in a cross-platform environment. The CI pipeline also includes a coverage test which measures how much of the code is really covered by the unit tests, the results are hosted by Codecov[7] and an error will be raised if the overall coverage is decreased by a pull request.

The CI pipelines are complemented by Continuous Delivery (CD) pipelines, which automatically build new Python wheels and send them to PyPI when a new version tag is pushed on the repository. CD pipelines are similar to CI pipelines, but are more constrained: they must provide release/optimized code which can be distributed. This is in particular a constraint for Linux environment where PyPi requires using a specific Linux Image, called *manylinux*, with a limited set of libraries that are expected to be found in any Linux environment. Finally, the documentation host is also part of the CD pipeline as it will automatically rebuild and publish a new version of the documentation when a new version tag is pushed.

Strategy and Roadmap. From the previous technical choices describing the project, several key strategies were put in place.

Adding New Features. Our strategy was to ship new features as fast as possible to quickly get users feedback. In practice, coding represents only about 25% of the time required to propose a new feature. The rest of the work corresponds to an investment of about 35% for writing tests and debugging, 30% for documentation and examples (notebooks), and 10% for the management of the project (updating libraries, updating CI/CD...).

Getting Users. Initially, the library project was shared with a few close users, which had the advantage of quick feedback, numerous bug fixes, and fairly frequent breaking changes. After this start-up period, we started to use the library extensively in courses, tutorial and research projects. We also took the habit to systematically publish companion notebooks based on the library to advertise and enhance the reproducibility of our research papers. Today the library is used

---

[5] https://readthedocs.org/.

[6] https://pypi.org/.

[7] https://about.codecov.io/.

in several labs, by researchers from the community and from other communities, essentially for some image processing methods that do not exist in more standard packages. In the future, we hope that some of these new users will contribute to the development of the library itself.

Global Feedback. The creation and the diffusion of this library is a very positive experience. In the same way as reported in the previous section, the library greatly eased several research projects within and outside our laboratory, as it saved a lot of time for interns and PhD students. It also greatly facilitates the dissemination of code and the reproducibility of our research papers.

4 Advanced Editorial Efforts

In this section, we discuss two RR platforms, which are managed by some of the authors of this article, showing the last editorial efforts to improve reproducible publications. These platforms do not consider the article itself as the sole output of the research work, but also include source code, rich interactive interfaces for demonstration, or even advanced system which go beyond the concept of simple and isolated demonstrators.

The two platforms we review are: a mature journal, IPOL, and a starting project which can be considered as its spin-off for industrial applications on machine learning (ML) algorithms, OVD-SaaS.

4.1 Improvements in the IPOL Journal

IPOL is a research journal on reproducible algorithms, focusing on their mathematical details [26]. It started as an image-processing journal, but soon it added other data types, such as video or audio, among others, as well as other applications, including remote sensing [27] or even biomedical [28], among others.

IPOL has continued to advance in making the system more adapted to the needs of authors and demo editors. Here we focus on three aspects and present what was done to improve the journal: the possibility to use a git repository to develop the code and see the results immediately in the online demonstration website, the use of containers for better reproducibility and maintenance, and new datatypes such as interactive maps for remote sensing applications.

Fast Development After Integrating Git. One request made to IPOL by authors was the possibility of fast code edition. Indeed, the IPOL editor or advanced users usually had to package their sources in a single file and upload it to some server; the IPOL's demo system would then download it, compile it, and run the updated version. The editors and authors felt that this was too time-consuming and preferred a solution more suited to their rapid development needs. Ideally, they wanted to use their own git repositories (for example, hosted in Github or Gitlab) and that the system fetched the last changes before each execution. This is now implemented in the system.

This brings up the question of reproducibility, given that, as authors are the owners of their repositories, they can change the published code at any moment. The solution adopted by IPOL is to let authors use their own repository, and at the moment of the publication, their repository is forked in a repository owned by IPOL. The code is then frozen at the particular revision which passed the peer review.

This is an example on how the source code is now specified in the demo description:

```
"build": {
    "url": "git@github.com:mlbriefs/88.git",
    "rev": "42252c0a84771c9abb141d0eacb6e9d54f44e9e5",
    "dockerfile": ".ipol/Dockerfile"
}
```

It specifies the git repository, a particular revision, and a Dockerfile. The use of Docker container in the demos is explained in the following section.

Execution in Docker Containers. When IPOL was started in 2009, C and C++ were some of the few accepted languages, along MATLAB. Authors were given strict coding guidelines and were limited to use a small subset of libraries known for their stability and backward compatibility. Indeed, most of the demos of that time are still running without major problems.

However, it was complicated to run MATLAB with a unique version of the framework, especially when authors actually used different versions, not necessarily the one accepted by IPOL. At the same time, Python gained a wide popularity in scientific research, and with the rise of machine learning and associated frameworks and libraries (PyTorch, TensorFlow, and others) it became the *de facto* standard.

Each MATLAB program could be designed to run on its own MATLAB version, and Python's virtual environments were not enough to ensure long term reproducibility. Indeed, it could happen that after a major update of the Debian distribution of the IPOL servers, some packages in PyPI were not yet available, among other causes that prevented reconstructing the same environment.

The solution that we adopted was to run the demos inside Docker containers. To make them reproducible, we maintain the complete instructions to re-create the container. Now all new IPOL demos are containerized, and we actively port the old ones to the new execution environment, now well-defined. We also expect that the use of containers will make it easier to run demos on the cloud in the future, combined with Infrastructure as Code techniques.

Interactive Map GeoJSON Demos. The opening of IPOL to more diverse research fields required to improve its underlying infrastructure to support new data types, especially in the web interface. In particular, IPOL has already published several articles on remote sensing, along with the associated demos [27].

One request from users and authors was the possibility to draw one or more polygonal regions on a map and to save them in the standard GeoJSON format (standardized by the IETF as RFC 7946).

A good library to render maps on websites was started by the Mapbox company in 2010, initially under a BDS license. On December 2021, the BSD license used in Mapbox GL JS was changed to a proprietary one. The community forked the project and started a free-software alternative, Maplibre, under BSD license again. Both projects have a very similar API. In 2023 we implemented the interactive map feature in IPOL, with Maplibre as the preferred option, to keep the project free software, although Mapbox is technically viable. Figure 6 shows a detail of an IPOL demo with this new feature.

The latitude and longitude of the polygon vertices is encoded in the GeoJSON response without further processing needed from the IPOL's side. It is also simple to obtain both the pixel locations and their corresponding longitude and latitude.

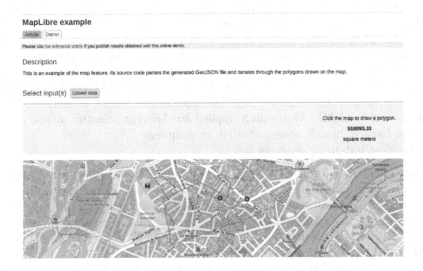

Fig. 6. A detail of an IPOL demo with a new feature: interactive map. In this example, one region has been already completed, and the second is being drawn. The feature is based on Maplibre and it allows to draw one or more regions as polygons on the map, and return them encoded in GeoJSON format.

Perpetual Archiving. Software as a fundamental artifact of the research must be perpetually preserved. Especially in the case of IPOL publication, where we consider the article, associated data, and source code as a whole.

Until 2020, IPOL simply stored in their own infrastructure the source code package which was accepted by the editors. The compromise of IPOL is to make the sources available forever, or at least for all the lifetime of the journal. However, the role of IPOL is not being a perpetual archive of source code. Note that, even large source code repositories such as Github, should be considered development tools, without that perpetual archiving commitment.

Fortunately, the Software Heritage project [29], supported by UNESCO, is devoted to the long-term preservation of software artifacts. Moreover, Software Heritage is able to point to the artifacts at different levels, such as package, git project, a particular commit, or even a specific line of the source code, thanks to the SWHID (SoftWare Hash IDentifier). The SWHID are intrinsic, persistent, and decentralized identifiers.

Since June 2020, IPOL systematically submits the source code of all published articles to Software Heritage[8], in an alliance in favor for Open Science and reproducibility.

4.2 OVD-SaaS, a Spin-Off of IPOL for Industrial Applications

OVD-SaaS (Online Verifiable Datascience Software as a Service) is a new project at Centre Borelli which can be considered as the extension of IPOL to industrial applications. This project takes advantage of the 12 years of experience with the current computing infrastructure of IPOL to develop a new general platform for artificial intelligence (AI), including machine learning (ML) applications.

OVD-SaaS aims at integrating diverse domains such as academic research, scientific publishers, and industry through the seamless end-to-end deployment of scalable, secure, reproducible industrial applications. This is expected to highlight the value of ML/AI research applied to different scientific fields, as for example finance, health, transportation, or commerce.

The most important features are:

– Easy comparison of algorithms on user data to establish the state of the art on diverse applications and datasets with a high level of confidentiality.
– A step to certification (badges) or at least granting a label of quality to algorithms, thus allowing for a better recognition and reputation for authors.
– High degree of specialization and standardization in peer-reviews of code for ML/AI scientific journals and conferences.
– Use of advanced cloud computing platform for end-to-end deployment of agile ML-Ops applications, from their publication in the scientific journal to their implementation at the operational level.
– Code provenance traceable, reproducible, citable (using SWHIDs) functionality by chaining algorithms to develop complete pipelines that provide support solutions to business problems across application domains.

The two main possible business models are:

– Sharing the responsibilities in reproducibility of scientific results, facilitating contracts between research laboratories, faculties and companies. This allows to develop specific algorithms which are relevant to their business or to benefit from the experience of the laboratory when jointly developing a complete pipeline.

---

[8] https://www.softwareheritage.org/2020/06/11/ipol-and-swh/?lang=es.

– Spin-off projects (startups or incubated within larger companies) which would design tailor-made software solutions for SMEs based on particular chains of algorithms optimized for specific businesses. It can be understood as an accelerator for the development of business ideas in startups by facilitating agile cycles providing proofs of concept, sandbox, and minimum viable products (MVP).

OVD-SaaS Applications. The OVD-SaaS application differs from the IPOL demo system in that it allows for applications whose lifetime is much larger compared to the short execution of an online demo. In the case of an online demonstration, the input data is loaded, the algorithm is run, the results are displayed, and the execution of the demonstration finishes. However, in the case of OVD-SaaS applications, they run continuously, listening for events to wake up and processes more data if needed. We shall generically call these new long-lived processes *Applications*. The architecture of the OVD-SaaS system has not been written from scratch, but new modules are added to the IPOL's architecture to build OVD-SaaS.

The main advantages of OVD as a SaaS system are the scalability of the application (permitting to spawn effortlessly new processing instances as needed) and the modularity of the resulting pipeline (permitting to replace any block with ease). The developer of an algorithm does not license its use to a client, instead it sells the service of processing the data, or a final application, as in our proposal.

5 Conclusion

Reproducible research is necessary for the advancement of science and the validation of research results. It requires efforts covering various fields including platforms to demonstrate and reproduce results, libraries to directly exploit research artifacts, and editorial work, publishing not only source code, but even complete services. We have surveyed different platforms which can be helpful in reproducible research, recent image-processing libraries such as Higra, and even journals such as IPOL. The IPOL was one of the first requesting that the article, the software and the associated data artifacts should be part of the same publication. IPOL is constantly adapting to the needs of its users with the inclusion of new data types and interactive visualizations. Inspired by IPOL, OVD-SaaS is an extension which intends to be a nexus between academy, industry, and publishers to provide an answer to the reproducibility problems in the context of industrial applications.

Strong efforts are needed from the different actors involved in the research community, such as authors, editors, and publishers. As we showed in this short survey, fortunately several tools, libraries, and services are available to help perform reproducible research.

Acknowledgement. The authors would like to thank Burak Yildiz from Delft University of Technology for providing statistics on reproducedpapers.org platform and Dean Pleban from the Dagshub platform for helping and orienting the authors to measure user activity. They also thank the reviewers for their valuable comments and corrections and Bruno Levy for pointing us the usage statistics of the Geogram Library.

References

1. Donoho, D.L., Maleki, A., Ur Rahman, I., Shahram, M., Stodden, V.: Reproducible research in computational harmonic analysis. Comput. Sci. Eng. **11**(1), 8–18 (2009)
2. Colom, M., Kerautret, B., Krähenbühl, A.: An overview of platforms for reproducible research and augmented publications. In: Kerautret, B., Colom, M., Lopresti, D., Monasse, P., Talbot, H. (eds.) RRPR 2018. LNCS, vol. 11455, pp. 25–39. Springer, Cham (2019). https://doi.org/10.1007/978-3-030-23987-9_2
3. Yildiz, B., et al.: ReproducedPapers.org: openly teaching and structuring machine learning reproducibility. In: Kerautret, B., Colom, M., Krähenbühl, A., Lopresti, D., Monasse, P., Talbot, H. (eds.) RRPR 2021. LNCS, vol. 12636, pp. 3–11. Springer, Cham (2021). https://doi.org/10.1007/978-3-030-76423-4_1
4. Lucic, A., Bleeker, M., Jullien, S., Bhargav, S., de Rijke, M.: Reproducibility as a mechanism for teaching fairness, accountability, confidentiality, and transparency in artificial intelligence (2022)
5. Rampin, R., Chirigati, F., Steeves, V., Freire, J.: ReproServer: making reproducibility easier and less intensive (2018). https://arxiv.org/abs/1808.01406
6. Rampin, R., Chirigati, F., Shasha, D., Freire, J., Steeves, V.: ReproZip: the reproducibility packer. J. Open Source Softw. **1**(8), 107 (2016)
7. Šimko, T., Heinrich, L., Hirvonsalo, H., Kousidis, D., Rodríguez, D.: REANA: a system for reusable research data analyses. In: EPJ web of conferences, vol. 214, p. 06034. EDP Sciences (2019)
8. Bonneel, N., Coeurjolly, D., Digne, J., Mellado, N.: Code replicability in computer graphics. ACM Trans. Graph. **39**(4), 93-1 (2020)
9. Stojnic, R., Taylor, R.: Papers with code-a facebook AI project (2018). https://paperswithcode.com. Accessed 30 Aug 2022
10. Bradski, G.: The OpenCV library. Dr. Dobb's J. Softw. Tools (2000)
11. McCormick, M., Liu, X., Jomier, J., Marion, C., Ibanez, L.: ITK: enabling reproducible research and open science. Front. Neuroinf. **8**, 13 (2014)
12. Rusu, R.B., Cousins, S.: 3D is here: point cloud library (PCL). In: IEEE International Conference on Robotics and Automation (ICRA). IEEE (2011)
13. The CGAL Project. CGAL User and Reference Manual. 5.4.1 edition (2022)
14. Tschumperlé, D.: The CIMG library. In: IPOL 2012 Meeting on Image Processing Libraries, p. 4 (2012)
15. Geogram: a programming library with geometric algorithms. https://github.com/BrunoLevy/geogram
16. Roynard, M., Carlinet, E., Géraud, T.: An image processing library in modern C++: getting simplicity and efficiency with generic programming. In: Kerautret, B., Colom, M., Lopresti, D., Monasse, P., Talbot, H. (eds.) RRPR 2018. LNCS, vol. 11455, pp. 121–137. Springer, Cham (2019). https://doi.org/10.1007/978-3-030-23987-9_12
17. Auber, D.: Tulip-a huge graph visualization framework. In: Graph Drawing Software, pp. 105–126. Springer, Heidelberg (2004). https://doi.org/10.1007/978-3-642-18638-7_5

18. Vigra: Vision with generic algorithms. https://ukoethe.github.io/vigra. Accessed May 2022
19. Dgtal: Digital geometry tools and algorithms library. http://dgtal.org
20. Moulon, P., Monasse, P., Perrot, R., Marlet, R.: OpenMVG: open multiple view geometry. In: Kerautret, B., Colom, M., Monasse, P. (eds.) RRPR 2016. LNCS, vol. 10214, pp. 60–74. Springer, Cham (2017). https://doi.org/10.1007/978-3-319-56414-2_5
21. Tierny, J., Favelier, G., Levine, J.A., Gueunet, C., Michaux, M.: The topology ToolKit. IEEE Trans. Vis. Comput. Graph. (2017). https://topology-tool-kit.github.io/
22. Perret, B., Chierchia, G., Cousty, J., Guimarães, S.J. F., Kenmochi, Y., Najman, L.: Higra: hierarchical graph analysis. SoftwareX **10**, 1–6 (2019). https://github.com/higra/Higra
23. Harris, C.R., et al.: Array programming with NumPy. Nature **585**(7825), 357–362 (2020)
24. Lam, S.K., Pitrou, A., Seibert, S.: Numba: a llvm-based python jit compiler. In: Proceedings of the Second Workshop on the LLVM Compiler Infrastructure in HPC, pp. 1–6 (2015)
25. Jakob, W., Rhinelander, J., Moldovan, D.: pybind11—seamless operability between c++11 and python (2016). https://github.com/pybind/pybind11
26. Nicolaï, A., et al.: The approach to reproducible research of the image processing on line (ipol) journal. Informatio **27**(1), 76–112 (2022)
27. Colom, M., Dagobert, T., Franchis, C.D., Gioi, R.G.V., Hessel, C., Morel, J.M.: Using the ipol journal for online reproducible research in remote sensing. IEEE J. Sel. Topics Appl. Earth Obs. Remote Sens. **13**, 6384–6390 (2020)
28. Baron, A.-F., Boulant, O., Panico, I., Vayatis, N.: A compartmental epidemiological model applied to the Covid-19 epidemic. Image Process. Line **11**, 105–119 (2021). https://doi.org/10.5201/ipol.2021.323
29. Di Cosmo, R., Zacchiroli, S.: Software heritage: why and how to preserve software source code. In: iPRES 2017–14th International Conference on Digital Preservation, pp. 1–10 (2017)

Reproducible Research Results

Enhancing GNN Feature Modeling for Document Information Extraction Using Transformers

Mouad Hamri[1,2]([✉]), Maxime Devanne[1], Jonathan Weber[1], and Michel Hassenforder[1]

[1] IRIMAS, University of Haute-Alsace, Mulhouse, France
{maxime.devanne,jonathan.weber,michel.hassenforder}@uha.fr
[2] Syentys, Brunstatt-Didenheim, France
mouad.hamri@uha.fr, mouad.hamri@syentys.fr
https://www.syentys.fr/

Abstract. Business documents are used every day by all kinds and sizes of companies and administrations, even if most of these entities have several information systems where the documents are digitilized in different formats (json, xml, database tables, ...), there still an important number of business documents that require manual processing which costs a lot and is very time consuming.

Extracting key-value information from business documents is a challenging problem due to the variety of document types and templates, in this work we will deal with the problem as a graph node classification problem using a multi "graph transformer" layers, we propose a graph construction method that focuses on the most relevant neighbours of every node while reducing the size of the graph and we use a document transformer embedding combined with some spatial and textual feature to give a better representation to each node.

Our contribution in this work was to conceive a graph neural network (GNN) achieving the highest results comparing to the rest of GNN models dealing with the same problem to our knowledge, the model is small (53,6K parameters) comparing to the recent models using transformers architectures (hundreds of millions of parameters) which is very suitable for applications when storage constraints are present, it also has a limited impact on the environment and represent an alternative to build greener AI systems.

We experiment our model on the SROIE ICDAR receipts dataset where we got an important F1 score compared to other graph neural network (GNN) based models.

Keywords: Document information extraction · GNN · Transformers

1 Introduction

Form-like documents as invoices, purchase orders and tax forms are massively used in day-to-day business workflow. Almost every company is receiving many

B. Kerautret et al. (Eds.): RRPR 2022, LNCS 14068, pp. 25–39, 2023.
https://doi.org/10.1007/978-3-031-40773-4_2

documents (sale orders, invoices) from their suppliers and from their customers (purchase orders) on a periodical basis, some of their employees are also sending each month the receipts corresponding to their different expenses (business trips, business lunches, ...).

The processing of these document is a time consuming task as a human intervention is needed to enter every document information in the business software of the company. The automation of this task will reduce the time and the cost of processing and will help a lot companies that are receiving a huge number of business documents every month.

Regular expression, heuristics and rules patterns were initially adopted to handle this task and were requiring a big effort and time to train the models to perform well for large varieties of document templates.

Recently the development of deep learning disciplines (CNN, RNN, LSTM, GRU, Transformers, GNN, ...) offered an opportunity to conceive better models giving better results with less effort that generalise better for unseen templates.

In this paper we propose an architecture composed of multiple GNN layers having as an input the nodes features representations, the output of the GNN is used as input to a feed-forward classifier, we experimented the model on the ICDAR SROIE [26] receipt dataset.

In the next section we will present the background and the related works. In Sect. 3 we will describe the document representation as graph. In Sect. 4 we will present the results and we will conclude with the perspectives.

2   Related Works

The problem of extracting key-value information such as date, supplier name and amount or even table items key-values (e.g. invoice lines: description, quantity, unit amount, ...) is an old problem that has gained a lot of interest in the recent years as many big companies have involved their R&D teams in conceiving robust and accurate architecture to deal with the problem as Google [10], SAP [12], Adobe [14], Alibaba [15] and Microsoft [16,17].

The algorithms dealing with document information parsing that have been conceived many decades ago (80s and 90s of the last century) was basically trying to code some rules using heuristics to predict the information of the document. One of the successful algorithm published in the 90s was the spectrum method [1] based on bottom-up, nearest-neighbour clustering of page components.

Another work was published based on top-down method that recursively split a document into column blocks and tokens [7].

These methods require a lot of human intervention (setting rules, ...) and often fail to generalise to unseen documents. Hence, it was inevitable to conceive new models based on machine learning technics that use the document structure and its text features to offer a tool that can generalise on unseen templates without any additional efforts.

The development of machine learning models and the breakthrough achievements of deep learning in the last two decades have pushed the researchers to conceive more powerful and performant architectures to extract structured information from documents.

Traditional neural networks like multilayer perceptron (MLP) [3] were initially adopted to solve this problem with a limited capability to handle this task as they ignore many aspects (visual features, document structure, poor text embedding representation, ...). Convolutional neural network (CNN) [2] allowed to obtain a representation that takes into account the visual features of an object (images, documents, ...). This allowed to achieve better results comparing to MLP.

But in order to get better results, the visual features are not sufficient as the document contains text and numerical data so the Natural Language Processing (NLP) [8] deep learning field gave a solution to capture these kind of features as it was very successful in dealing with texts and sequences data in general.

Many works [9,11–14] used both visual and text embedding in addition to some spatial features as the bounding boxes coordinates to ensure a good representation of the document. However, the fact that these representations are processed independently and the results are concatenated in a later stage didn't allow to have a high performance (the performance is still very high compared to CNN models or NLP models).

Vaswani et al. [4] presented in 2017 a breakthrough architecture they called "The transformers" based on the "attention" mechanism, this idea has helped to achieve better results than the state-of-the-art models at that time and reduced drastically the computing time as the operations involve matrix multiplications that can be ran in parallel to benefit from the power of GPUs (Graphics processing unit) or TPUs (Tensor Processing Unit), this was the beginning of a new era and many other transformers architectures were published.

One of theses transformers was BERT (Bidirectional Encoder Representations from Transformers) [5] which is an encoder, the main idea behind the BERT transformer is to generate a representation from "Pre-training" tasks and then use this representation in the "Fine-tuning" step to handle various downstream tasks.

Microsoft has published a model [16] called LayoutLM where they introduced an architecture based on the transformers model, the architecture is based on the BERT model where a faster R-CNN model [22] is used to inject a visual embedding to capture the visual informations. The model was compared to a standard BERT/RoBERTa [6] models, the authors have already assessed the performance of many variants of their model by tweaking some hyper-parameters.

A second version "LayoutLMv2" was later proposed in [17], the new architecture integrates the document text, layout and image information in the pre-training stage. It also added text-image matching and text-image alignment as new pre-training strategies to enforce the alignment among different modalities.

Graph neural networks (GNN) raised a lot of interest in the last few years as it allows to address some problems that traditional models can not handle efficiently.

The main idea behind GNN is the construction of a graph where for each node the neighbours are passing a message using a specific aggregation function. Many layers can be stacked to ensure the propagation of features from the deep neighbours, a new architecture of "Convolutional graph neural networks" was introduced in [18], a new approach for message passing aggregation was proposed in [19], the attention mechanism to calculate weights of neighbours messages was integrated in [20] and the transformers architecture to conceive a "graph transformer" was adopted in [21].

The problem of classifying document fields deals with a 2D structure as each element is defined by its text and by its spatial attributes (x and y positions, size of the field, ...). Each element may also have neighbours in the four directions: up, down, left and right. So applying an NLP approach which works greatly for 1D sequential text won't be able to capture the spatial dimension nor the fields neighbourhood. That is why the representation of the document using a graph is a better approach as the graph will preserve the document structure. The graph representation is much more efficient compared to a vision pixel-grid representation (CNN) dealing with the boxes as images as the storage of the graph requires less memory comparing to the document image pixels.

The usage of a GNN model to extract document information has been already adopted in many works. Authors of [24] and authors of [25] proposed two GNN models, the first based on Chebyshev graph convolutional neural networks [27] and the second on the Graph Attention Network (GAT) [28] where they stacked multiple layers in both models followed by a feed-forward classifier. They constructed the node features by concatenating 3 types of features: text, layout and other features [24, 25]. The text features are the result of BPEmb embeddings [29] where the text is splited into 3 words to get at the end a vector of dimension 300 (each word embedding is a vector of dimension 100). They formed the graph in [24] by choosing the 4 nearest neighbours and in [28] by forming a star sub-graph neighborhood for each node where they consider the boxes that are within an area of a certain dimensions.

GNN presents a suitable approach to represent documents as it allows to preserve its structure. In general, the document texts are represented as nodes and the spatial relationships are presented as edges (neighborhood).

In our approach, we propose a GNN model using a rich encoder transformer representation as we believe that it is a perfect candidate to build an efficient feature vector for the graph node as it combines the bounding box, the image and the text to create the embedding vectors comparing to the only usage of text representation as proposed by [24, 25]. For the edge construction, we propose to link each node with a maximum number of 4 edges where we also limit the vertical neighbours to the upper and lower lines. This will lead to smaller graphs which will present a big advantage when dealing with larger datasets and richer documents.

3   Proposed Model

Our proposed model follows the steps illustrated in the Fig. 1 The first step "Texts and bounding boxes" consist in getting the document texts with the corresponding bounding boxes using an OCR (optical character recognition), in the second step "Features assignment" we assign to each text/bounding box a feature vector (represented by the colored boxes in the pipeline figure), in the third step "Graph construction" we create the document graph, in the fourth step "GNN model" we construct the GNN model that has the document graph created in the previous step as input and in the last step "Model prediction" we generate the prediction output in json format with the predicted value of each keyword. The different steps are described in detail in the next subsections.

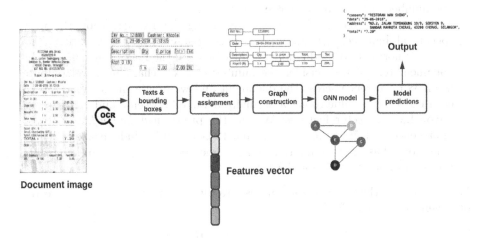

Fig. 1. Pipeline of our model

3.1   Texts and Bounding Boxes

Each document image is processed by an OCR that returns the set of document texts with the corresponding bounding boxes $(t^i, x_1^i, x_2^i, y_1^i, y_2^i)$ where t^i is the text and $(x_1^i, x_2^i, y_1^i, y_2^i)$ are the coordinates of the box i ($i \in [1, n]$ where n is the number of document texts). As we will see in the coming sections, we evaluate our model against SROIE [26] dataset where the bounding boxes for the training and testing datasets are given but any OCR such as $Tesseract^1$ can be used to get the bounding boxes and the corresponding texts.

---

[1] https://github.com/tesseract-ocr/tesseract.

In addition to the elements got from the OCR step, we assign to each element (text/bounding box) the box line number as well. By the end of this step, we get a list of the document texts with three attributes for each element (text, bounding box, line number).

3.2 Features Assignment

We assign a feature vector to each extracted text/bounding box from the previous step. The features are assigned as follow:

- Spatial features: a vector of 3 floats composed of the normalised coordinates of the box center: x_{center}/w and y_{center}/h ((x_{center}, y_{center}) are the coordinates of the box center while w and h are the width and height of the image respectively) and the normalized box line number: l_{box}/L (l_{box} is the box line number and L is document number of lines).
- Text features: a vector of 6 floats representing the number of lower, upper, special, alphanumeric, numeric and space characters in the box text. The vector is normalized by dividing each element by the max occurrence in the document (e.g. if we consider the number of lower characters, we compute the max occurrence across the document and we divide the number got for each box by this value to get a normalized value between 0 and 1).
- LayoutLM v2 vector features: We use the pre-trained *LayoutLM V2* base model encoder [17] having 12 layers and 12 heads with a hidden size of d=768 (the model has approximately 200M parameters)[2], this gives an embedding vector of dimension 768 for the box.

We concatenate the three vectors and as a result, each node has a feature vector of dimension 777 (see Fig. 2)

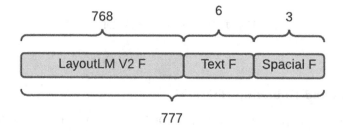

Fig. 2. Feature vector of dimension 777

3.3 Graph Construction

Each document in the dataset is represented by an undirected graph $\mathcal{G}(N, E)$ (N is the set of nodes and E is the set of edges). The graph is constructed using output of the previous steps where each box represents a graph node (see Fig. 3) having the computed feature vector.

---

[2] https://huggingface.co/docs/transformers/model_doc/layoutlmv2.

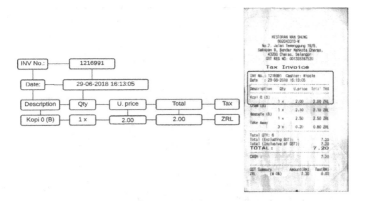

Fig. 3. Example of graph construction of a receipt sub-region

For each boxes we consider the 4 nearest neighbours in the four directions: up, down, left and right. For the up and down neighbours we consider only the boxes belonging to the previous or next line number (if the box line number is l, we link only if the neighbour line number l' satisfies : $l - 1 \leq l' \leq l + 1$, this constraint ensures that for the vertical neighbours, we create a link if only the difference between the neighbour line number and the line number doesn't exceed 1). This will ensure that a box in the header will not be linked to a box in the footer of the document if there's no other boxes between them vertically (see Fig. 4 and Fig. 5).

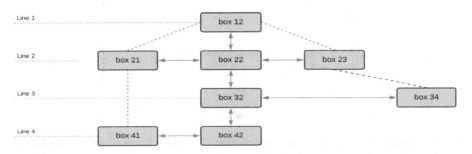

Fig. 4. Example of graph neighbours selection. The "box 22" has 4 neighbours (top, bottom, left and right) while the "box 21" has only 1 neighbour (right), the "box 21" can not be a neighbour of the "box 41" as the difference between their line numbers is greater than 1 (line 2 and line 4)

So by the end of this process each box will have a left neighbour (if it exists), a right neighbour (if it exists), an upper neighbour (if it exists and if the difference between their line numbers is less or equal than 1) and a bottom neighbour (if it exists and if the difference between their line numbers is less or equal than 1) which assigns to it a maximum of 4 neighbours.

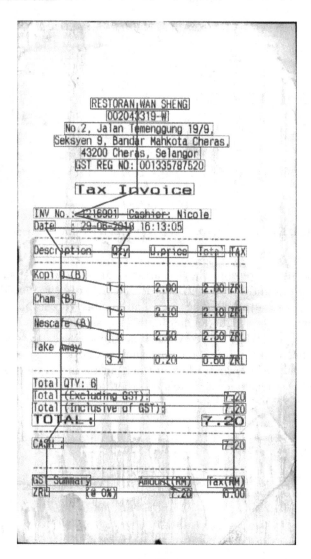

Fig. 5. Example of a receipt graph construction. The black boxes represent the nodes the blue arrows show the up/down edges and the red arrows the left/right. (Color figure online)

3.4   GNN Model

As mentioned previously, the transformer architecture [4] has given great results to NLP tasks, we adopted the same philosophy and we chose the transformer operator [21] for our GNN model. This operator was called "transformer" as its idea is inspired from the transformer architecture.

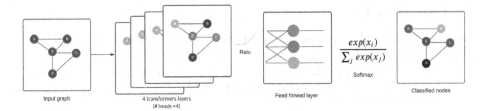

Fig. 6. Model architecture

The proposed model has multiple layers of "graph transformers" [21] with a Relu activation function after each layer followed by a feed-forward layer with a softmax for the classification (see Fig. 6).

The input of the network is the set of nodes features detailed in the Sect. 3.2 $H^{(0)} = \{h_1^{(0)}, h_2^{(0)}, ..., h_n^{(0)}\}$ where n is the number of graph nodes. The representation of the layer l: $H^{(l)} = \{h_1^{(l)}, h_2^{(l)}, ..., h_n^{(l)}\}$ is obtained by applying a multi-head attention [4] (C is the number of heads).

For each head c and nodes i, j, the attention coefficients are computed as follow:

$$\alpha_{c,ij}^{(l)} = \frac{\langle q_{c,i}^{(l)}, k_{c,j}^{(l)} \rangle}{\sum_{u \in \mathcal{N}(i)} \langle q_{c,i}^{(l)}, k_{c,u}^{(l)} \rangle}$$

where $\mathcal{N}(i)$ is the neighbours set of the node i, q and k are the query and key [4] tensors obtained by applying a linear transformation on the node features (trainable matrices), $\langle q, k \rangle = exp(\frac{q^T k}{\sqrt{d}})$ where d is the hidden size of each head (we omitted the edge features as they are not applied in our case).

We the get our message aggregation by concatenating the C heads attention:

$$v_{c,j}^{(l)} = W_{c,v}^{(l)} h_j^{(l)} + b_{c,v}^{(l)}$$

$$\hat{h}_i^{(l+1)} = \|_{c=1}^{C} \left[\sum_{j \in \mathcal{N}(i)} \alpha_{c,ij}^{(l)} v_{c,j}^{(l)} \right]$$

the $\|$ symbol is the concatenation operator, W is a trainable weight and b is a trainable bias.

The output of the last layer is the average of the multi-head output, the authors have also proposed a gated residual connection between the layers to prevent the model from over-smoting.

3.5   Model Prediction

In the final step of our pipeline, the trained model is used to predict the document fields where the output is a json file with the values of the predicted fields.

4   Experiments

We experiment field extraction by evaluating four variants of feature architectures against our proposed model to study the effect of using a rich representation. In the following subsections we will present the dataset, the followed experimental setup, the metrics and the obtained results.

4.1   Dataset

The dataset used is the SROIE [26] receipt dataset containing 626 documents for training and 347 for testing.

Each document has a file image (jpeg format), a json file containing the value of each field (the fields are: company, address, date and total) and a file containing the bounding boxes of the document with the text of each box.

As the bounding box files are not labelled, we start by labelling the train and test datasets where we assign a class for each box, we assign also to each box its line number in the document. As there are some mistakes in the original dataset [35], we re-created the json files of the test dataset.

4.2   Experimental Setup

We compare the results for our model (we will call it LM777) with 4 other variants where for the first one we replace the LayoutLMv2 representation with BERT[3] [5] representation (same dimension 777) that we call BERT777, for the second one we use only the LayoutLMv2 representation (dimension 768) that we call LM768, for the third one we use only the BERT representation (dimension 768) that we call BERT768, and for the last one we consider only the spatial and textual features (dimension 9) that we call ST9 (The proposed representation and their variants are summarized in Fig. 7)

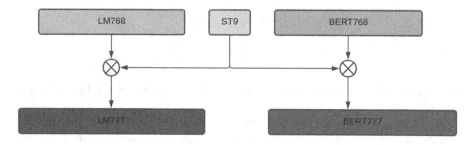

Fig. 7. Features variants: LM777 is the combination of LM768 and ST9 while BERT777 is the combination of BERT768 and ST9

We have used 20% of the training dataset for validation and we performed a K-Fold cross validation (K = 5), we also run several experiments using 5 different seeds to validate the reproducibility of the results.

---

[3] https://huggingface.co/docs/transformers/model_doc/bert.

4.3 Metrics

The metrics used to assess the model performance were the precision, the recall and the F1 score. As a reminder the precision, the recall and F1 score are calculated as follow: $F1 = \frac{2*P*R}{P+R}$ where: $P = \frac{TP}{TP+FP}$ and $R = \frac{TP}{TP+FN}$ (P: precision, R: recall, TP: True Positive, TN: True Negative, FP: False Positive and FN: False Negative)

For each document in our test dataset, we generate as an output a json file containing the extracted fields (company, address, date and total), for the company and address, we concatenate the texts of the predicted boxes (boxes predicted as members of the field class) to get the final value while for the total and date, we consider the boxes having the higher probability (among the members of the field class). The metrics are computed based on the extracted fields in comparison with the ground truth values by using the SROIE results script[4] that compare the json results.

4.4 Results

The Table 1 presents the precision, recall and F1 scores of our model compared to the other variants where we report the best F1 score of each variant.

As we performed K-Fold cross validation and ran the experiments over different seeds, we report the mean μ and the standard variation σ of the F1 metric for each variant.

Table 1. Precision, Recall and F1 scores result on SROIE dataset of our model compared to the other variants. The bold values represent the higher results

Model	Precision	Recall	F1	μ (F1)	σ (F1)
LM777	**0,9542**	**0,9191**	**0,9363**	0,9132	0,0084
BERT777	0,9467	0,9104	0,9282	0,9111	0,0092
LM768	0,9533	0,9003	0,9260	0,9106	0,0072
BERT768	0,9505	0,9025	0,9259	0,9113	0,0096
ST9	0,8601	0,7818	0,8195	0,8009	0,0114

We can see that the ST9 model has the worst results which clearly shows that using only some spatial and textual features is not enough to achieve great results. However their injection in combination with LayoutLMv2 or BERT representation allowed to improve the results in comparison with the only usage of LayoutLMv2 or BERT representations.

The best model was LM777 followed by BERT777, LM768, BERT768 and finally ST9 which confirms that combining LayoutLMv2 and BERT representation with spatial and textual features would give the higher scores and that LayoutLMv2 representation is richer and better than BERT representation.

---

[4] https://rrc.cvc.uab.es/?ch=13&com=downloads.

SROIE task 3 competition [26] is maintaining a results broad where the best performances are reported. In comparison with models using purely GNN, our results are better than [25] that has the best published F1 score for a GNN model on SROIE dataset to our knowledge. (The authors of [34] used a GNN but they combined it's embedding with text and image embeddings and feed the result to a BiLSTM-CFR layers).

At the time of this writing, among the top 3 performers ,the only paper available is the paper of the Top 1 model [31] (not a GNN architecture), their authors conceived a multi-layer transformer where they included a multi-modal feature enhance module, they pre-trained their module on DOCBANK [32] and RVL-CDIP [33] datasets which contain 500K document pages and 400k grayscale images in 16 classes, with 25k images per class respectively.

The Top 3 models are performing better than our model but we think that our model presents some advantages as it was trained only on 500 receipt (80% of SROIE training dataset) and has 53,6K parameters while the Top 1 was pre-trained on 900k documents and has 107M of parameters (even if we use LayoutLMV2 model in the feature assignment phase, we train only 53,6K parameters). We believe that training our model on larger dataset of more large number of templates will help to achieve better results.

4.5 Implementation Details

We implemented our model using *Pytorch Geomtric* library[5] and *networkx* for the graph construction.[6]. The model training and testing were done using *Pytorch Lightning* library[7]. The training was done using mini-batches on a 2000 epochs with an early stopping strategy (patience of 200 epochs), based on a Grid Search analysis we used the following hyper-parameters: 4 layers of "graph transformers" with 4 heads of a hidden size of 16 for each head, we used the ADAM optimizer with a learning rate of 0,001 and a weight decay of 5×10^{-4} and we applied of dropout of 0,1.

5   Conclusion

We presented in this paper a graph neural network model to label Form-like documents fields. We proposed an optimized method to construct the document graph while having smaller graphs, we used a rich node embedding based on LayoutLMv2 [17] representation combined with spatial and textual features and we used multiple graph transformer layers [21] to force the model to focus on the most relevant neighbours. We achieved an F1 score of 0,9363 on SROIE dataset which is the best result achieved using a purely GNN model to our knowledge. Our model has only 53,6K parameters which make it very suitable to situations where the storage is a constraint and it also has a lower carbon

---

[5] https://pytorch-geometric.readthedocs.io/en/latest.

[6] https://networkx.org.

[7] https://www.pytorchlightning.ai.

footprint comparing the majority of models dealing with the same problem. In our future works, we will try to procure or generate larger datasets to give our model the chance to achieve higher scores as it was trained on a very small number of document (500 documents). We will also try to conceive new graph convolutional layers suitable for document information extraction problem while fine-tuning the features and graph architectures.

We will also consider different type of business documents like CVs and payslips and work on more advanced problems such as tables and lines detection and parsing.

References

1. O'Gorman, L.: The document spectrum for page layout analysis. IEEE Trans. Pattern Anal. Mach. Intell. **15**(11), 1162–1173 (1993). https://doi.org/10.1109/34. 244677
2. LeCun, Y., et al.: Gradient-based learning applied to document recognition. Proc. IEEE 86(11), 2278–2324 (1998)
3. Haykin, S.: Neural Networks: A Comprehensive Foundation. Prentice Hall PTR, Upper Saddle River (1994)
4. Vaswani, A., et al. Attention is all you need (2017). arXiv:1706.03762 [cs]
5. Devlin, J., Chang, M.W., Lee, K., Toutanova, K.: BERT: pre-training of deep bidirectional transformers for language understanding (2019). arXiv:1810.04805 [cs]
6. Liu, Y., et al.: RoBERTa: a robustly optimized BERT pretraining approach (2019). arXiv:1907.11692 [Cs]
7. Ha, J., Phillips, I.T., Haralick, R.M.: Document page decomposition using bounding boxes of connected components of black pixels. In: Document Recognition II, vol. 2422, pp. 140–151. International Society for Optics and Photonics (1995). https://doi.org/10.1117/12.205816
8. Socher, R., Bengio, Y., Manning , C.D.: Deep learning for NLP (without magic). In: Tutorial Abstracts of ACL 2012, ACL 2012, vol. 5. Association for Computational Linguistics (2012)
9. Palm, R.B., Laws, F., Winther, O.: Attend, copy, parse end-to-end information extraction from documents. In: 2019 International Conference on Document Analysis and Recognition (ICDAR), pp. 329–336 (2019). https://doi.org/10.1109/ ICDAR.2019.00060
10. Majumder, B.P., Potti, N., Tata, S., Wendt, J.B., Zhao, Q., Najork, M.: Representation learning for information extraction from form-like documents. In: Proceedings of the 58th Annual Meeting of the Association for Computational Linguistics, pp. 6495–6504. Association for Computational Linguistics (2020). https://doi.org/10.18653/v1/2020.acl-main.580. https://www.aclweb.org/ anthology/2020.acl-main.580)
11. Patel, S., Bhatt, D.: Abstractive information extraction from scanned invoices (AIESI) using end-to-end sequential approach (2020). arXiv:2009.05728
12. Katti, A.R., Reisswig, C., Guder, C., Brarda, S., Bickel, S., Höhne, J., Faddoul, J.B.: Chargrid: towards understanding 2D documents. In: Proceedings of EMNLP, pp. 4459–4469 (2018)

13. Denk, T.I., Reisswig, C.: BERTgrid: contextualized embedding for 2D document representation and understanding. In: Workshop on Document Intelligence at NeurIPS 2019 (2019)
14. Davis, B., Morse, B., Cohen, S., Price, B., Tensmeyer, C.: Deep visual template-free form parsing. In: ICDAR, pp. 134–141 (2019)
15. Liu, X., Gao, F., Zhang, Q., Zhao, H.: Graph convolution for multimodal information extraction from visually rich documents. In: Proceedings of the 2019 Conference of the North American Chapter of the Association for Computational Linguistics: Human Language Technologies, vol. 2 (Industry Papers), pp. 32–39. Association for Computational Linguistics, Minneapolis . https://doi.org/10.18653/v1/N19-2005
16. Xu, Y., Li, M., Cui, L., Huang, S., Wei, F., Zhou, M.: Layoutlm: pre-training of text and layout for document image understanding. In: Proceedings of the 26th ACM SIGKDD International Conference on Knowledge Discovery and Data Mining (2020)
17. Xu, Y., et al.: LayoutLMv2: multi-modal pre-training for visually-rich document understanding (2011). arXiv:2012.14740 [cs]
18. Kipf, T.N., Welling, M.: Semi-supervised classification with graph convolutional networks (2017). arXiv:1609.02907 [cs, stat]
19. Hamilton, W.L., Ying, R., Leskovec, J.: Inductive representation learning on large graphs (2018). arXiv:1706.02216 [cs, stat]
20. Veličković, P., Cucurull, G., Casanova, A., Romero, A., Liò, P., Bengio, Y.: graph attention networks (2018). arXiv:1710.10903 [cs, stat]
21. Shi, Y., Huang, Z., Feng, S., Zhong, H., Wang, W., Sun, Y.: Masked label prediction: unified message passing model for semi-supervised classification (2021). arXiv:2009.03509 [cs, stat]
22. Ren, S., He, K., Girshick, R., Sun, J.: Faster R-CNN: towards real-time object detection with region proposal networks. In: Proceedings of the 28th International Conference on Neural Information Processing Systems (NIPS 2015), vol. 1, pp. 91–99. MIT Press, Cambridge (2015)
23. Riba, P., Dutta, A., Goldmann, L., Fornés, A., Ramos, O., Lladós, J.: Table detection in invoice documents by graph neural networks. In: 2019 International Conference on Document Analysis and Recognition (ICDAR), pp. 122–127 (2019). https://doi.org/10.1109/ICDAR.2019.00028
24. Lohani, D., Belaïd, A., Belaïd, Y.: An invoice reading system using a graph convolutional network. In: Carneiro, G., You, S. (eds.) ACCV 2018. LNCS, vol. 11367, pp. 144–158. Springer, Cham (2019). https://doi.org/10.1007/978-3-030-21074-8_12
25. Belhadj, D., Belaïd, Y., Belaïd, A.: Consideration of the word's neighborhood in GATs for information extraction in semi-structured documents. In: Lladós, J., Lopresti, D., Uchida, S. (eds.) ICDAR 2021. LNCS, vol. 12822, pp. 854–869. Springer, Cham (2021). https://doi.org/10.1007/978-3-030-86331-9_55
26. Huang, Z., et al.: ICDAR2019 competition on scanned receipt OCR and Information extraction. In: 2019 International Conference on Document Analysis and Recognition (ICDAR), pp. 1516–1520 (2019). https://doi.org/10.1109/ICDAR.2019.00244
27. Defferrard, M., Bresson, X., Vandergheynst, P.: Convolutional neural networks on graphs with fast localized spectral filtering. In: Advances in Neural Information Processing Systems, pp. 3844–3852 (2016)
28. Velickovic, P., Cucurull, G., Casanova, A., Romero, A., Lio, A., Bengio, Y.: Graph attention networks. In: Proceedings of ICLR, pp. 1–12 (2017)

29. Heinzerling, B., Strube, M.: BPEmb: tokenization-free pre-trained subword embeddings in 275 languages. In: Proceedings of the 11th International Conference on Language Resources and Evaluation (2018)
30. Kipf, T.N., Welling, M.: Semi-supervised classification with graph convolutional networks. In: International Conference on Learning Representations (ICLR) (2017)
31. Li, Y., et al.: StrucTexT: structured text understanding with multi-modal transformers (2021). arXiv:2108.02923 [cs]
32. Li, M., et al.: DocBank: a benchmark dataset for document layout analysis (2020). arXiv:2006.01038 [cs]
33. Harley, A.W., Ufkes, A., Derpanis, K.G.: Evaluation of deep convolutional nets for document image classification and retrieval. In: ICDAR (2015)
34. Yu, W., Lu, N., Qi, X., Gong, P., Xiao, R.: PICK: processing key information extraction from documents using improved graph learning-convolutional networks (2004). arXiv:2004.07464 [cs]
35. Tchoubith, N., Calusha, P.: ICDAR 2019 robust reading challenge on scanned receipts OCR and information extraction (2021). https://github.com/BlackStar1313/ICDAR-2019-RRC-SROIE

Short ICPR Companion Papers

A Novel Pattern-Based Edit Distance for Automatic Log Parsing: Implementation and Reproducibility Notes

Maxime Raynal[1,2]([✉]), Marc-Olivier Buob[1], and Georges Quénot[2]

[1] Nokia Bell Labs, Massy, France
marc-olivier.buob@nokia-bell-labs.com
[2] University Grenoble Alpes, CNRS, Grenoble INP, LIG, 38000 Grenoble, France
maxime.raynal@gmail.com, georges.quenot@imag.fr

Abstract. This paper presents a detailed and reproducible description of the algorithms and experiments published in our ICPR paper (*A novel pattern-based edit distance for automatic log parsing*). It discusses the implementation, our methodology, our experimental setup, the considered performance metrics and the influence of the main parameters of the compared algorithms.

Keywords: Edit distance · log clustering · dynamic programming · reproducible research

1 Introduction

Unstructured data is ubiquitous, and its lack of structure makes it difficult to analyze. As a sequel, it often ends up being unused [20]. In practice, processing unstructured data forces to develop dedicated parsers to convert it to a more convenient and structured format. This problem arises in network management, especially when analyzing system *logs*[1] or system command outputs. Unfortunately, developing parsers is often tedious, time consuming and error prone.

To automate log parsing, it is required to better understand the structure of the file that must be processed. In the literature, grouping the lines of a log having the same underlying structure and semantics is often referred to as the *log clustering* (and sometimes, *log parsing*) problem. To solve this problem, we propose in [19] a novel pattern-based distance and a clustering algorithm built on top of it [17]. As a result, our clustering algorithm partitions input log lines so that each group of lines conforms to a same underlying structure (*template*). It worth noting that the templates are not known *a priori* and are inferred during the log clustering step.

This companion paper details how to reproduce our experiments. Section 2 explains some of our implementation choices. Section 3 describes how to install, setup and use our module through a minimal example. Section 4 recalls the main

---

[1] Logs are text files, where each line usually corresponds to a timestamped message.

B. Kerautret et al. (Eds.): RRPR 2022, LNCS 14068, pp. 43–50, 2023.
https://doi.org/10.1007/978-3-031-40773-4_3

steps of our algorithm and details how to tune each hyper-parameter. Section 5 presents how we compared though experiments our proposal against two state of the art solutions and discusses the influence of each hyper parameter. Section 6 concludes the paper.

2   Implementation Considerations

The `pattern clustering` code architecture involves C++ and Python 3 code. The core algorithm is implemented in C++, while the Python wrapping eases its usage. Implementing the core algorithm in C++ improves the performance of the pattern clustering by a factor of 100 compared to a pure Python implementation, and hence allows to process larger log files. The Python wrapping is realized thanks to `libpython` and the `Boost.python` libraries [4]. As the module includes a C++ core, once compiled, the `pattern_clustering` module only works for the python version corresponding to the `libpython` and `Boost.python` libraries we linked to.

We could have restricted to `libpython`, but we decided to also rely on the Boost library for two reasons. First, `Boost.python` allows to keep the C++ core independent from the implementation details imposed by `libpython`. Second, wrapping C++ objects usable from the python interpreter imposes to build the appropriate `libpython` objects. This task is significantly eased by using the `Boost.python` library.

In our case, the `pattern_distance` and `pattern_clustering` primitives take in parameter pattern automata and vectors [19]. All these variables are represented C++-side by using `std::vector` instances. As vectors are not handy to craft automata, we require an intermediate automaton-like class. We could have used `Boost.graph`, but for sake of simplicity, we kept the graph aspects in the Python part of module.

To do so, we decided to use the `pybgl` Python module [3] for two reasons. First, `pybgl` provides an automaton class that can easily extended to implement pattern automata. Second, it provides all the primitives required to build an automaton from an arbitrary regular expression. The Python/C++ bindings enable transparent conversions between Python objects and C++ objects. In the details, Python pattern automata and Python lists are converted to C++ vectors. Conversely, the C++ vectors involved in the results are converted to Python lists.

Note that our implementation does not use GPU. The computed clustering does not depend on the versions of the project dependencies nor the hardware used to run the experiments.

3   Installation Steps

The installation steps are described in the wiki of the `pattern_clustering` repository [17]. The installation of the `libboost-dev` and `libpython3-dev` libraries is explained. Unfortunately, the PIP-based installation [18] is not yet

```
1  from pattern_clustering import pattern_clustering
2
3  FILENAME = "/var/log/Xorg.0.log" # Or any arbitrary log file
4  with open(FILENAME) as f:
5      LINES = [line.strip() for line in f.readlines()]
6
7  print(pattern_clustering(LINES))
```

Fig. 1. Minimal example using the `pattern_clustering` function.

available as it would require to compile a version for every target operating system and Python version. Doing so is not straightforward, even using projects like ManyLinux [2], and that is why we decided to provide only a source-based installation.

Once installed, the end-user can run the minimal example provided in Fig. 1. To obtain more user-friendly results, we refer the user to the Jupyter notebooks provided in the `pattern_clustering` repository.

4 Pattern Clustering Usage

This section presents the parameters of our module and more advanced usages than the one provided in Fig. 1. It also discusses how to tune each hyper-parameter if the default settings are not satisfactory.

As explained in [19], the `pattern_clustering` primitive takes the following parameters:

- `lines`: an iterable object (e.g., a `list`) of strings corresponding to each input log line. As the pattern clustering algorithm is greedy, one could pass an iterator allowing to process an input log file in a streaming fashion.
- `map_name_dfa`: a dictionary mapping pattern names with the corresponding deterministic finite automaton (DFA). In [19], this corresponds to the pattern collection denoted by $\mathcal{P}$. We detail this parameter in Sect. 4.1.
- `densities`: the density of each pattern is a value between 0 and 1 reflecting how strict is a pattern. In [19], this corresponds to results returned by the density function ρ. The vector of densities offers the opportunity to use alternative density functions.
- `threshold`: this value, between 0 and 1, indicates how close must be the elements involved in a cluster from the cluster's representative. In [19], this corresponds to D. Small values tend to increase the number of output clusters.
- `use_async`: a Boolean indicating whether the pattern clustering computations must be parallelized.
- `make_mg`: the strategy used to build pattern automata from string according to $\mathcal{P}$. Each input log line is converted to its corresponding pattern automaton by extending the **grep** algorithm (based on Thompson algorithm [21]) that we call "multi grep" (in short, "mg"). The resulting pattern automaton is minimal finite w.r.t. the alphabet defined by $\mathcal{P}$. Doing accelerates enables

optimization to check whether two pattern automata are equal. The end-user must keep the default value to conform to our reproduce the pattern automata simplifications and experiments presented in [19].

The value returned by the `pattern_clustering` primitive is detailed in Sect. 4.2. Finally, Sect. 4.3 presents two ways to perform the clustering.

4.1 Pattern Collection

In our implementation, each pattern is identified by a string. Some patterns are predefined in our module. The whole list of supported patterns may be obtained by running the snippet reported in Fig. 2:

```
1 from pattern_clustering import get_pattern_names
2 print(get_pattern_names())
```

Fig. 2. Snippet to list the predefined patterns.

By default, the pattern collection involves most of them. One may tune this collection by discarding some keys, modifying some automata, or injecting custom patterns. The snippet reported in Fig. 3 shows how to inject a custom pattern named `letters` in the default collection. In the details, the `compile_dfa` processes the input regular expression using the Shunting Yard algorithm [5]. By using the Thompson transformation [21], it progressively builds a non-deterministic finite automaton (NFA). Finally, the NFA is transformed to its corresponding minimal DFA using the Moore algorithm [13].

```
1 from pattern_clustering import *
2 from pybgl.regexp import compile_dfa
3
4 MAP_NAME_DFA = make_map_name_dfa()
5 MAP_NAME_DFA["letters"] = compile_dfa("[a-zA-Z]+")
6 print(pattern_clustering(LINES, map_name_dfa=MAP_NAME_DFA))
```

Fig. 3. Snippet to tune the pattern collection.

4.2 Returned Value

Once the clustering is computed, each input line is remapped with the appropriate cluster. The `pattern_clustering` returns a list where each element represents a cluster. The ith element of this list gathers the line number of the lines belonging to the ith cluster.

4.3   Dropping Duplicated Pattern Automata

Our module allows to drop duplicated pattern automata. This feature is relevant if the end-user considers that every line conforming to the same pattern automaton must always fall in the same cluster. Dropping duplicated pattern automata limits the number of elements to cluster and thus accelerates the processing.

However, we did not use this feature in our experiments. Indeed, we observed that it could affect the quality of the clustering, as in some situations, two lines conforming to the same pattern automaton should fall in distinct clusters.

5   Experimental Setup

In [19], we compare the pattern clustering against two state-of-the-art algorithms, namely Drain [8] and LogMine [7]. Our experimental setup is quite similar to the one described in [22]. This section details the main differences.

5.1   Drain and LogMine Integration

The standard implementations of Drain [12] and LogMine [6] do not output the cluster assigned to each input log line. This information is required to compute the accuracy (see Sect. 5.5). That is why we have forked these standard implementations and adapted their outputs [14,15]. Our modifications are minor: we just slightly enriched the results returned by Drain and LogMine so that we can compare the performance of the different proposals. Thus, they do not affect the results and only induce negligible time overhead.

5.2   Loghub Dataset

We perform our experiments on the Loghub dataset. It involves 16 log files described in detail in [10] (size, number of messages, labeling, etc.). The Loghub repository [9] provides a small excerpt of each log file, whereas the Zenodo repository [1] contains the complete logs.

5.3   Ground Truth

The Loghub repository [9] provides for each log file the corresponding ground truth. A ground truth maps templates (i.e., a string involving some wildcards denoted by <*>) with the corresponding lines of log.

It's worth noting that each ground truth has been manually obtained. During our experiments, we have observed they contain several inconsistencies. In particular, we have found some clusters that have no reason to be split. For example, the original *Android* ground truth distinguishes the three following templates:

```
- animateCollapsePanels:flags=<*>,
  force=false, delayed=false, mExpandedVisible=false
```

```
- animateCollapsePanels:flags=<*>,
  force=false, delayed=false, mExpandedVisible=true
- animateCollapsePanels:flags=<*>,
  force=true, delayed=true, mExpandedVisible=true
```

... while it would be more natural to merge them in a single template:

```
- animateCollapsePanels:flags=<*>,
  force=<*>, delayed=<*>, mExpandedVisible=<*>
```

We have checked each ground truth and fixed all the inconsistencies we have found. The original and the fixed versions of the ground truths are made available in [16]. One may easily compare them using a `diff`-like utility. All our experiments are performed using the fixed ground truths.

5.4   Experimental Parameters

The three considered clustering algorithms mainly require two parameters, namely the pattern collection and the clustering threshold.

For each dataset, our experiments consider two pattern collections:

- *Minimal collection.* Our initial motivation is to design a generic log clustering tool, and thus this collection only includes universal patterns (i.e., patterns like dates, times, network addresses, numerical values).
- *Specific collections.* In [22], the authors tailor dataset-dependant to see how good each algorithm with a high prior knowledge could be. As a sequel, the resulting collection is highly dependent on the input dataset and requires significant end-user intervention.

To get a full benchmark, our experiments compare the results obtained for each dataset with the specific and the minimal collections.

As done in [22], the threshold is calibrated by running the experiments with several values. We keep the best results obtained w.r.t the tested thresholds.

To make our experiments easily reproducible, all the simulation parameters are made available in our repository. We also provide notebooks allowing to run our experiment pipeline.

5.5   Accuracy

The accuracy of each clustering algorithm is evaluated by computing two performance metrics (namely, the parsing accuracy and the adjusted Rand index). Both require a ground truth (see Sect. 5.3).

The *parsing accuracy* has been introduced in [22].

More formally, given two partitions C_1, C_2 of a set E, the pattern accuracy PA is defined by:

$$PA(C_1, C_2) = \frac{1}{|E|} \sum_{C \in C_1 \cap C_2} |C|$$

By definition, this metric only rewards clusters that *exactly* matches those listed in the ground truth. As a sequel, if a cluster is slightly different in the results and in the ground truth, this is not rewarded by PA; and the bigger the cluster, the bigger the penalty. This means that algorithms returning a clustering with small errors may have a very low parsing accuracy. Conversely, slight updates modifying a large cluster in the ground truth drastically change the parsing accuracy.

The adjusted Rand index [11] is designed to be less sensitive to small variations and hence alleviates all the limitations inherent to the parsing accuracy. Intuitively, it is obtained by counting the number of correct and incorrect *pairwise assignments* and is readjusted depending on the number of clusters and their respective size.

6 Conclusion

This companion paper shows how to reproduce the experiments presented in [19] and highlights some of its technical contributions. First, it details the code optimizations (core algorithm written in C++, parallelization) made to run our algorithm on larger logs (made a few thousands of lines). Second, it shows the effort made to package the code, so that it is easy to install and use for the end-user. Third, it provides all the technical material needed to reproduce our experiments, and hence allows researchers to compare their proposal against LogMine, Drain and the pattern clustering algorithm. Fourth, it has been the opportunity to enhance the ground truths provided by the Loghub dataset and to use them in our experiments. For all these reasons, we hope that our module will be reused in the future works dealing with log clustering and automatic parsing.

References

1. Anonymous: Zenodo repository containing the full Loghub logs. https://zenodo.org/record/3227177
2. Authority, P.P.: ManyLinux GitHub repository. https://github.com/pypa/manylinux
3. Buob, M.O.: PyBGL GitHub repository. https://github.com/nokia/pybgl
4. community, B.: Boost C++ library. https://www.boost.org/
5. Dijkstra, E.W.: Algol 60 translation: An algol 60 translator for the x1 and making a translator for algol 60. Stichting Mathematisch Centrum. Rekenafdeling (1961). https://www.cs.utexas.edu/EWD/MCReps/MR35.PDF
6. Dinh, T.: Logmine original repository. https://github.com/trungdq88/logmine/
7. Hamooni, H., Debnath, B., Xu, J., Zhang, H., Jiang, G., Mueen, A.: Logmine: Fast pattern recognition for log analytics. In: Proceedings of the 25th ACM International on Conference on Information and Knowledge Management, pp. 1573–1582 (2016)
8. He, P., Zhu, J., Zheng, Z., Lyu, M.R.: Drain: An online log parsing approach with fixed depth tree. In: 2017 IEEE International Conference on Web Services (ICWS), pp. 33–40. IEEE (2017)

9. He, S., Zhu, J., He, P., Lyu, M.R.: Loghub: A large collection of system log datasets for AI-powered log analytics. https://github.com/logpai/loghub
10. He, S., Zhu, J., He, P., Lyu, M.R.: Loghub: A large collection of system log datasets towards automated log analytics. arXiv preprint arXiv:2008.06448 (2020)
11. Hubert, L., Arabie, P.: Comparing partitions. Journal of classification **2**(1), 193–218 (1985)
12. LOGPAI: Drain 3 original repository. https://github.com/IBM/Drain3
13. Moore, E.F., et al.: Gedanken-experiments on sequential machines. Automata Studies **34**, 129–153 (1956)
14. Raynal, M.: Drain 3 forked repository. https://github.com/raynalm/Drain3
15. Raynal, M.: Logmine forked repository. https://github.com/raynalm/logmine
16. Raynal, M., Buob, M.O., Quénot, G.: Ground truth templates. https://github.com/nokia/pattern-clustering/tree/main/notebooks/experiments_icpr
17. Raynal, M., Buob, M.O., Quénot, G.: Pattern clustering GitHub repository. https://github.com/nokia/pattern-clustering
18. Raynal, M., Buob, M.O., Quénot, G.: Pattern clustering on PyPI. https://pypi.org/project/pattern-clustering/
19. Raynal, M., Buob, M.O., Quénot, G.: A novel pattern-based edit distance for automatic log parsing. In: ICPR 2022 (2022)
20. Terrizzano, I.G., Schwarz, P.M., Roth, M., Colino, J.E.: Data wrangling: The challenging yourney from the wild to the lake. In: CIDR (2015)
21. Thompson, K.: Programming techniques: regular expression search algorithm. Commun. ACM **11**(6), 419–422 (1968)
22. Zhu, J., et al.: Tools and benchmarks for automated log parsing. In: 2019 IEEE/ACM 41st International Conference on Software Engineering: Software Engineering in Practice (ICSE-SEIP), pp. 121–130. IEEE (2019)

Companion Paper: Deep Saliency Map Generators for Multispectral Video Classification

Jens Bayer[1,2]([✉]) [iD], David Münch[1,2] [iD], and Michael Arens[1,2] [iD]

[1] Fraunhofer Center for Machine Learning, Sankt Augustin, Germany
[2] Fraunhofer IOSB, Gutleuthausstr. 1, 76275 Ettlingen, Germany
`jens.bayer@iosb.fraunhofer.de`

Abstract. This is the companion paper for the ICPR 2022 Paper "Deep Saliency Map Generators for Multispectral Video Classification", that investigates the applicability of three saliency map generators on multispectral video input data. In addition to implementation details of modifications for the investigated methods and the used neural network implementations, the influence of the parameters and a more detailed insight in the training and evaluation process is given.

Keywords: Reproduction Paper · Saliency · Video Classification

1 Introduction

Providing the source code not only gives a better understanding of the statements, it also helps to verify the outcomes of the examined experiments. Nonetheless, even the best-documented source code can still leave questions unanswered, such as how a specific parameterization changes the results or why a selected metric was chosen. In the following, a more detailed view on the examined saliency map generators (Sect. 2) of the addressed Paper [1] is given. In addition, the influence of the methods' parameters regarding the deletion and insertion metric is shown. Afterwards, the used network implementations are described (Sect. 3). The last section covers the evaluation with the used metrics (Sect. 4).

Our source code can be found at GitHub[1] and requires Python 3.9, PyTorch 1.8.2 LTS, and torchvision 0.9.

2 Deep Saliency Map Generators

The three investigated methods are Grad-CAM [4], Randomized Input Sampling for Explanation (RISE) [3] and the similarity difference and uniqueness method (SIDU) [2]. Since they are usually applied to ordinary images, some adjustments have been made, that are explained in the following. For Table 1 and Table 2, ↑ (↓) indicates, that a higher (lower) value is better.

---

[1] https://github.com/JensBayer/ICPR2022.

B. Kerautret et al. (Eds.): RRPR 2022, LNCS 14068, pp. 51–56, 2023.
https://doi.org/10.1007/978-3-031-40773-4_4

2.1 Grad-CAM

While Grad-CAM not only outperforms its competitors, it is also the simplest to implement. Grad-CAM generates a saliency map by calculating a weighted sum of the forward features of the last convolutional layer. The weights are determined by the gradient of the target class. Grad-CAM requires a forward and backward pass of the input through the network. We therefore register a forward and backward hook at the target layer of our model, to extract the forward features F and the gradient $G^c = \frac{\partial y^c}{\partial F_k}$ for the score y^c of the target class c. Here, k equals the number of forward feature maps, generated by the network. The gradient is summed to obtain the neuron importance weights

$$\alpha_k^c = \sum_{i,j} G_{kij}^c \tag{1}$$

as described by [4]. The forward features are multiplied with the neuron importance weights and activated via ReLU. The final saliency map

$$S^c = upscale(ReLU(\sum_k \alpha_k^c F_k)) \tag{2}$$

is given by the upscaled weighted sum of the features. Since 3D ResNet generates three-dimensional forward features, the temporal dimension must also be taken into account in Eq. 1. Additionally, the bilinear interpolation in Eq. 2 changes to a trilinear interpolation.

2.2 RISE

RISE is a Monte Carlo approach that masks the input and calculates a weighted sum of the masks according to the output of the masked input to retrieve a saliency map. For RISE, we largely stick to the official implementation[2]: First, $n = 1000$ random binary grids of size $s = 2 \times 8 \times 8$ are sampled in such a way, that the value of a tile of the grid equals one with a probability of $p = 0.1$. Each grid is either bilinear or trilinear, upscaled to a slightly larger size than the input. The resulting grids are randomly cropped to match the input size. After this, the input data is multiplied elementwise with these masks and propagated through the network. The resulting network output P is then used as a weighting term in the calculation of the final saliency map:

$$S^c = \sum_k^n P_k^c \cdot crop(upscale(G_k)), \quad G_k \in \{0,1\}^s, \quad P(G_{kij} = 1) = p \tag{3}$$

As it can be seen in Table 1, the usage of more masks lead to slightly better Deletion and Insertion scores, but comes at the cost of a significant higher computation time. Furthermore, the temporal mask resolution with $s = 2 \times 8 \times 8$ leads in almost all cases to the best or tied to the best scores. The increased probability of $p = 0.25$ for a grid tile to be nonzero, has also a positive influence and leads to slightly better scores.

---

[2] https://github.com/eclique/RISE.

Table 1. Deletion and Insertion score for different parameters for RISE, using the IRTV trained network. Only a single parameter is modified, while the remaining two are set to the default values, described in Subsect. 2.2.

Image Spectrum	Parameters	3D-ResNet 18		PAN	
		Deletion ↓	Insertion ↑	Deletion ↓	Insertion ↑
TV	$n = 10^2$	0.18 ± 0.13	0.55 ± 0.23	0.27 ± 0.18	0.51 ± 0.22
	$n = 10^3$	$\mathbf{0.17 \pm 0.09}$	0.60 ± 0.24	0.22 ± 0.18	0.59 ± 0.22
	$n = 10^4$	0.18 ± 0.08	$\mathbf{0.62 \pm 0.24}$	$\mathbf{0.22 \pm 0.17}$	$\mathbf{0.61 \pm 0.24}$
IR	$n = 10^2$	0.18 ± 0.13	0.48 ± 0.27	0.17 ± 0.14	0.51 ± 0.23
	$n = 10^3$	0.16 ± 0.10	0.54 ± 0.26	0.16 ± 0.14	0.54 ± 0.23
	$n = 10^4$	$\mathbf{0.16 \pm 0.08}$	$\mathbf{0.57 \pm 0.26}$	$\mathbf{0.16 \pm 0.13}$	$\mathbf{0.55 \pm 0.23}$
TV	$s = 2 \times 8 \times 8$	0.18 ± 0.10	$\mathbf{0.64 \pm 0.20}$	0.23 ± 0.17	$\mathbf{0.58 \pm 0.24}$
	$s = 4 \times 8 \times 8$	0.18 ± 0.19	0.56 ± 0.22	0.24 ± 0.17	0.50 ± 0.23
	$s = 8 \times 8 \times 8$	$\mathbf{0.16 \pm 0.21}$	0.43 ± 0.30	0.26 ± 0.14	0.45 ± 0.22
IR	$s = 2 \times 8 \times 8$	0.18 ± 0.10	$\mathbf{0.61 \pm 0.23}$	$\mathbf{0.17 \pm 0.14}$	$\mathbf{0.54 \pm 0.22}$
	$s = 4 \times 8 \times 8$	$\mathbf{0.18 \pm 0.12}$	0.61 ± 0.24	0.18 ± 0.12	0.54 ± 0.24
	$s = 8 \times 8 \times 8$	0.18 ± 0.16	0.58 ± 0.23	0.22 ± 0.13	0.50 ± 0.23
TV	$p = 0.10$	0.18 ± 0.10	$\mathbf{0.61 \pm 0.23}$	0.23 ± 0.18	0.60 ± 0.23
	$p = 0.25$	$\mathbf{0.18 \pm 0.12}$	0.61 ± 0.24	$\mathbf{0.23 \pm 0.19}$	$\mathbf{0.66 \pm 0.24}$
	$p = 0.50$	0.18 ± 0.16	0.58 ± 0.23	0.27 ± 0.21	0.65 ± 0.26
IR	$p = 0.10$	0.18 ± 0.10	0.58 ± 0.23	$\mathbf{0.17 \pm 0.15}$	0.53 ± 0.23
	$p = 0.25$	$\mathbf{0.17 \pm 0.09}$	$\mathbf{0.59 \pm 0.23}$	0.17 ± 0.16	$\mathbf{0.62 \pm 0.23}$
	$p = 0.50$	0.18 ± 0.12	0.56 ± 0.24	0.19 ± 0.17	0.60 ± 0.24

2.3 SIDU

SIDU uses the features of the last convolutional layer to mask the input data, propagates the masked input through the network and calculates the similarity differences and a uniqueness scores of the output to finally generate a saliency map. As for RISE, we also stick largely to the official implementation of SIDU[3]. To extract the forward features, we register a forward hook at the target layer of the used model and perform a forward propagation. The network output $\tilde{P}$ and the forward features F are recorded. The masks

$$M = upscale(\tilde{M}), \quad \tilde{M}_{kij} = \begin{cases} 1 & \text{if } F_{kij} > \tau \\ 0 & \text{else} \end{cases} \tag{4}$$

are the result of the binarization of the forward features with a threshold ($\tau = 0.5$), followed by a bilinear or trilinear upscaling. Similar to RISE, the masks are elementwise multiplied with the input data and propagated through the network. The resulting network output P is used in the calculation of the similarity difference sd and uniqueness u scores. The resulting saliency map

$$S = u(P_k) \cdot sd(P_k, \tilde{P})) \cdot M_k \tag{5}$$

is the product of those two scores and the corresponding masks.

---

[3] https://github.com/satyamahesh84/SIDU_XAI_CODE.

Table 2. Deletion and Insertion scores for different τ values.

Image Spectrum	τ	3D-ResNet 18		PAN	
		Deletion ↓	Insertion ↑	Deletion ↓	Insertion ↑
TV	-1	0.35 ± 0.17	0.46 ± 0.19	0.40 ± 0.21	0.49 ± 0.22
	-0.5	0.35 ± 0.17	0.46 ± 0.19	0.40 ± 0.21	0.49 ± 0.22
	0	**0.18 ± 0.08**	**0.67 ± 0.18**	0.26 ± 0.14	0.62 ± 0.25
	0.5	0.18 ± 0.09	0.67 ± 0.18	0.23 ± 0.16	**0.68 ± 0.22**
	1	0.18 ± 0.09	0.67 ± 0.19	**0.23 ± 0.15**	0.68 ± 0.22
IR	-1	0.29 ± 0.15	0.42 ± 0.19	0.36 ± 0.18	0.48 ± 0.23
	-0.5	0.29 ± 0.15	0.42 ± 0.19	0.36 ± 0.18	0.48 ± 0.23
	0	0.17 ± 0.08	0.64 ± 0.20	0.21 ± 0.12	0.59 ± 0.24
	0.5	**0.17 ± 0.08**	**0.64 ± 0.20**	**0.18 ± 0.12**	**0.63 ± 0.21**
	1	0.17 ± 0.08	0.63 ± 0.20	0.18 ± 0.12	0.63 ± 0.21

Table 2 shows the influence of τ on the Deletion and Insertion scores. For $\tau \geq 0$, the Deletion and Insertion scores are quite similar.

3   Networks

The investigated network families are 3D-ResNets and the Persistent Appearance Networks (PAN). Since the Multispectral Action Dataset is comparably small, we used the 3D-ResNet 18 provided by torchvision and the official PAN-Lite network implementation[4].

3.1   3D-ResNet

The target layer for the forward feature extraction of Grad-CAM and RISE, when used with 3D-ResNets, is the output of the last convolutional layer right before the pooling layer. The upscaling for all three investigated methods is trilinear.

3.2   Persistent Appearance Network

Since we use PAN with a ResNet 50 backbone, the forward features are also extracted at the last convolutional layer right before the pooling layer. The upscaling, however, is bilinear for Grad-CAM and SIDU and trilinear for RISE. The trilinear upscaling provides a more temporally stable mask.

---

[4] https://github.com/zhang-can/PAN-PyTorch.

4   Evaluation

The experiments are evaluated with the Deletion and Insertion metric on sequences of the Multispectral Action Dataset. The fixed train and test split can be found in the git repository, while the dataset can be freely requested.

4.1   Deletion Metric

Given a saliency map $S \in \mathbb{R}^{t \times h \times w}$ and an input sequence $I \in \mathbb{R}^{t \times c \times h \times w}$, the Deletion metric (see Algorithm 1) first sorts the indices of the entries of S in descending order, according to their values. Afterwards, the sorted indices are separated in n coherent parts and the values of S are successively replaced with a fixed value $v = 0$, according to the partition order. After each part, the classifier f computes the class probability for the target class t of the modified input. The class probability after the ith part is recorded in p_i. Finally, the area under the curve of the entries of p and the linear spaced values from 0 to 1 in n steps is returned.

Algorithm 1. Deletion score calculation.

1: **function** DELETIONSCORE(f, S, I, n, v, t)
2:     $sorted\_idx \leftarrow argsort(S)$
3:     $parts \leftarrow split(sorted\_idx, n)$
4:     $p \leftarrow 0^n$
5:     **for** $i = 0, \ldots, n$ **do**
6:         **for all** $j \in parts_i$ **do**
7:             $I_j \leftarrow v$
8:         **end for**
9:         $p_i \leftarrow \sigma(f(I))_t$ ▷ σ is the softmax function
10:    **end for**
11:    $score \leftarrow AreaUnderCurve(p)$
12:    **return** $score$
13: **end function**

Algorithm 2. Insertion score calculation.

1: **function** INSERTIONSCORE(f, S, I, n, t)
2:     $sorted\_idx \leftarrow argsort(S)$
3:     $parts \leftarrow split(sorted\_idx, n)$
4:     $\tilde{I} \leftarrow blur(I)$
5:     $p \leftarrow 0^n$
6:     **for** $i = 0, \ldots, n$ **do**
7:         **for all** $j \in parts_i$ **do**
8:             $\tilde{I}_j \leftarrow I_j$
9:         **end for**
10:        $p_i \leftarrow \sigma(f(\tilde{I}))_t$
11:    **end for**
12:    $score \leftarrow AreaUnderCurve(p)$
13:    **return** $score$
14: **end function**

4.2   Insertion Metric

Similar to the Deletion metric, the Insertion metric (see Algorithm 2) successively unblurs a blurred version $\tilde{I}$ of the input data I, according to the importance score of the given saliency map S.

5   Conclusion

This paper shows the impact of different parameter choices for already existing methods, namely Grad-CAM, RISE and SIDU, when applied not to ordinary images but rather video input data in the visual and long-wave infrared spectrum. To quantify the results, the Deletion and Insertion metric are used. While for RISE, a higher number of generated masks seems to improve the scores, a higher temporal mask resolution seems to be counterproductive. The probability parameter used by RISE seems not to have a big impact. For SIDU, the default value for the threshold $\tau = 0.5$ results in most cases in the best or close to the best scores.

Acknowledgements. This work was developed in Fraunhofer Cluster of Excellence "Cognitive Internet Technologies".

References

1. Bayer, J., Munch, D., Arens, M.: Deep Saliency Map Generators for Multispectral Video Classification. In: 2022 26th International Conference on Pattern Recognition (ICPR), pp. 3757–3764. IEEE (8 2022). https://doi.org/10.1109/ICPR56361.2022.9955639. https://ieeexplore.ieee.org/document/9955639/
2. Muddamsetty, S.M., Mohammad, N.S.J., Moeslund, T.B.: SIDU: Similarity Difference And Uniqueness Method for Explainable AI. In: 2020 IEEE International Conference on Image Processing (ICIP), pp. 3269–3273. IEEE (10 2020). https://ieeexplore.ieee.org/document/9190952/
3. Petsiuk, V., Das, A., Saenko, K.: RISE: Randomized input sampling for explanation of black-box models. In: British Machine Vision Conference (BMVC) (2018)
4. Selvaraju, R.R., Cogswell, M., Das, A., Vedantam, R., Parikh, D., Batra, D.: Grad-CAM: visual explanations from deep networks via gradient-based localization. Int. J. Comput. Vision **128**(2), 336–359 (2019). https://doi.org/10.1007/s11263-019-01228-7

On Challenging Aspects of Reproducibility in Deep Anomaly Detection

Konstantin Kirchheim[✉], Marco Filax, and Frank Ortmeier

Otto-von-Guericke-University, Magdeburg, Germany
{konstantin.kirchheim,marco.filax,frank.ortmeier}@ovgu.de

Abstract. This companion paper focuses on challenging aspects of reproducibility that emerge in anomaly detection with Deep Neural Networks. We provide motivating examples based on our work and present mitigation strategies. Furthermore, we document a trade-off between the complexity of experiments and the strength of the empirical evidence obtained through them, both of which impact different types of reproducibility. Ultimately, we argue that the reproducibility of inferences should be prioritized over the reproducibility of exact numerical results.

Keywords: Reproducibility · Anomaly Detection · Deep Learning

1 Introduction

Reproducibility has been a source of debate in several scientific disciplines and recently gained more attention in the machine learning community, with some researchers proclaiming a reproducibility crisis [9]. Difficulties reproducing the methods, results, or findings of previous work with Deep Neural Networks (DNNs) have been reported in supervised, unsupervised, and reinforcement learning [2,6,12,14,15]. In this companion paper, we discuss challenging aspects of reproducibility that arise in anomaly detection with DNNs based on our work on Multi-Class Hypersphere Anomaly Detection (MCHAD) [10]. The source code is publicly available online[1]. We adopt the nomenclature introduced in [2], which identified three different types of reproducibility:

1. **Method Reproducibility**: reproducibility of the numerical results when the same code gets executed.
2. **Results Reproducibility**: reproducibility of statistically similar results when a method is reimplemented.
3. **Inferential Reproducibility**: reproducibility of findings or conclusions in different experimental setups.

---

[1] https://gitlab.com/kkirchheim/mchad.

© The Author(s), under exclusive license to Springer Nature Switzerland AG 2023
B. Kerautret et al. (Eds.): RRPR 2022, LNCS 14068, pp. 57–66, 2023.
https://doi.org/10.1007/978-3-031-40773-4_5

The remainder of this paper is structured as follows: In Sect. 2, we describe a common experimental setup used in anomaly detection with DNNs. In Sect. 3, we examine challenges for reproducibility arising in these experimental setups and common mitigation strategies. In Sect. 4, we discuss a trade-off between the complexity of the experiments and the strength of the empirical evidence obtained through them that emerges from the presented strategies.

2   Deep Anomaly Detection

Let the data points $\mathbf{x} \in \mathcal{X} \subset \mathbb{R}^n$ be drawn *i.i.d.* from a data generating distribution $p_{in}(\mathbf{x}, y)$ where $y \in \mathcal{Y}$ are class labels. The goal of anomaly detection can be described as detecting data points $\mathbf{x}$ that have low marginal probability (or no support) under p_{in}, i.e., all points in the set of anomalies $\mathcal{A} = \{\mathbf{x} \in \mathcal{X} : p_{in}(\mathbf{x}) \leq \alpha\}$ where $\alpha \in [0, 1]$ [16].

Training. In the cases we consider in this work, a neural network f with parameters θ is trained on some upstream task, for example, classification. Finding the optimal parameters of this network is performed by solving an optimization problem of a form similar to

$$\arg \min_{\theta} \mathbb{E}_{(\mathbf{x}, y) \sim p_{in}} \left[\mathcal{L}(f(\mathbf{x}; \theta), y) \right] \tag{1}$$

where $\mathcal{L}$ is some loss function and p_{in} is the data-generating distribution. Since the distribution is unknown, the optimization is usually performed empirically over some dataset $\mathcal{D}^{in}_{train} = \{x_n \sim p_{in}^i\}_{n=1}^{N}$ using some variant of stochastic gradient descent.

Detection. Deep Anomaly Detection can be approached by using the trained neural network f to construct a detector $D_f : \mathbb{R}^n \rightarrow \mathbb{R}$ that assigns outlier scores $D_f(\mathbf{x})$ to inputs. Anomalies can then be detected by applying a threshold $\tau \in \mathbb{R}$ as

$$\text{outlier}(x) = \begin{cases} 1 & \text{if } D_f(\mathbf{x}) > \tau \\ 0 & \text{else} \end{cases} . \tag{2}$$

Outlier Exposure. Recently, several methods have been proposed that include a sample dataset of anomalies $\mathcal{D}^{out}_{train} = \{x_n \sim p_{out}^{train}\} \subset \mathcal{A}$ into the training process. Such methods usually add a regularization term to eq. (1) that incentivises that the outlier scores $D_f(\mathbf{x})$ are more discriminative for normal points and anomalies [4,8,13].

Evaluation. In a common experimental setting, the performance of this detector is evaluated in a supervised manner by casting the detection as a binary classification problem and testing the ability of the detector to discriminate between a sample of $\mathcal{D}^{in} = \{\mathbf{x}_n \sim p_{in}\}_{n=1}^{N}$ and outlier dataset $\mathcal{D}^{out}_i = \{x_n \sim p_{out}^i\}_{n=1}^{N_i} \subset \mathcal{A}$ with $i \in \mathbb{N}$ where p_{out}^i are distributions from which the example anomalies are drawn. During the evaluation, the model $f(\cdot; \theta)$ is assigned a performance score $\mathcal{P}(f(\cdot; \theta), \mathcal{D}^{in}, \mathcal{D}_i^{out})$ for each $\mathcal{D}_i^{out}$. For multiple outlier datasets, the per-model results are averaged. The performance of binary classifiers can be measured by several metrics, for example, by threshold-independent metrics like the Area under the Receiver Operating Characteristic (AUROC) and the Area under the Precision-Recall Curve (AUPR) or the False Positive Rate that is achieved at a particular True Positive Rate.

3 Challenges for Reproducibility

In the following, we aim to outline challenging aspects of the reproducibility of experiments for anomaly detection with DNNs, as described above. For each of these identified challenges, we will present examples and briefly discuss the corresponding aspect of our own work.

3.1 Nondeterminism in Network Optimization

It has been repeatedly demonstrated that the optimization of DNNs is influenced by various sources of nondeterminism [2,12,15]. These include, among others, the network initialization, stochasticity in algorithms like dropout, the shuffling of the training data, and nondeterminism in low-level libraries like cuDNN [3] and random data augmentation. Furthermore, the optimization is sensitive to small changes in the initial conditions to such a degree that changing the least significant bit in the initialization of an optimization parameter results in a performance variance similar to that observed when using a completely different initialization [18].

As [2] argues, setting the random seed to a fixed value would also reduce the validity of conclusions drawn from such experiments to this particular random seed. Therefore, while eliminating all sources of randomness in experiments guarantees method reproducibility, it does not improve results- or inferential reproducibility.

Mitigation. A common strategy to address the performance variance is to treat the network optimization in (1) as a random process and to conduct repeated experiments with different random seeds (called seed replicates [2]). The corresponding performance measures can then be subjected to statistical tests to determine their consistency with the null hypothesis (that there is no performance difference

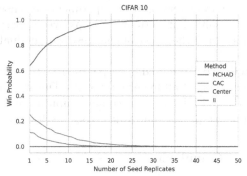

Fig. 1. Estimated probability of method having the highest average AUROC over a specific number of seed replicates of experiments on the CIFAR10 dataset.

between methods). While using statistical tests is a well-established practice in most empirical sciences, it is, to our knowledge, not applied consistently in the machine learning domain.

Example. We trained four different models 100 times, each with different random seeds on the CIFAR-10. Using Monte Carlo sampling, we can estimate the probability that a method will achieve the highest mean AUROC for a certain number of seed replicates N. The results are depicted in Fig. 1. For a small N, several methods have a substantial chance of having the highest average performance.

MCHAD. In our work, we ran experiments with $N = 21$ different random seeds to ensure the statistical robustness of the results. We chose this number not due to theoretical considerations but because we have access to 21 GPUs, which allows us to parallelize all trials from one model while fully utilizing the available resources. We publish the used random seeds with the source code to ensure the method reproducibility.

3.2 Sensitivity to Hyperparameters

Models based on DNNs can be sensitive to the choice of hyperparameters, and different models might require different hyperparameters on different datasets.

Example. We trained MCHAD models based on a DNN with varying capacity for 100 epochs without dropout on the CIFAR-10 dataset, each with the same random seed. The results are depicted in Figure 2. We observe that while higher model capacity correlates with performance on the classification task, slight changes to the DNN architecture can cause significant changes in performance measures for anomaly detection.

Mitigation These effects can be mitigated by performing extensive hyperparameter optimization, allocating an equal computational budget to each method to ensure a fair comparison [2], and publishing source code to disclose the exact hyperparameters used in experiments to ensure the reproducibility of methods and results. Furthermore, sweeps over hyperparameters can be used to help to understand the effect of changes in individual parameters.

MCHAD. We reused hyperparameters from the literature and performed manual fine-tuning of all hyperparameters. During training, we used the same backbone DNN and allocated an equal computational budget to each method. Furthermore, we publish our source code to disclose all hyperparameters.

3.3 Complexity

Implementations can contain errors, and larger codebases might be more difficult to understand and are, therefore, generally more prone to contain errors. In the same sense, datasets can contain "errors", for example, in the form of overlaps

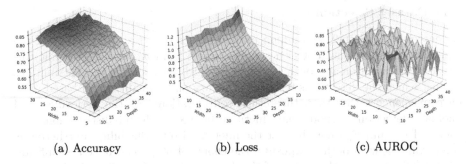

(a) Accuracy (b) Loss (c) AUROC

Fig. 2. Classification accuracy and anomaly detection AUROC of MCHAD for varying network widths and depths for a ResNet architecture [5], trained on the CIFAR-10 dataset. Anomaly detection performance averaged over seven different outlier datasets. Compared to the classification accuracy, the surface 2c is more erratic, indicating that slight changes in the DNN architecture can result in significantly different performance on the anomaly detection task. Note that we flipped the axis on Fig. 2b for better visibility.

between the training and test datasets (*target leakage*), and pre-trained weights could induce a bias, depending on the data that was used for training. Overlap between different datasets is particularly likely to occur when the datasets stem from similar distributions (with shared support), for example, when both were scraped from the internet.

Example. Re-using weights pre-trained on a downscaled version of the ImageNet dataset [7,17] could induce bias in our experiments since the classes of the ImageNet and the CIFAR classes overlap to a certain extent. Also, the 80 Million TinyImages database [19] that was often used as $\mathcal{D}_{train}^{out}$ is known to have semantic overlap with the CIFAR datasets.

Mitigation. Complexity can be outsourced to third-party libraries that have been reviewed by different individuals, which decreases the probability of undetected implementation errors. For model weights, the situation is more difficult since the parameters of DNNs can generally not be interpreted by humans. Instead, the training script should be scrutinized.

MCHAD. To keep our codebase small, we used existing libraries where possible. Our source code (transiently) depends on 212 Python packages, including `pytorch-ood` [11], which contains tested implementations of several anomaly detection methods, datasets and pre-trained weights. We also provide instructions for replicating the execution environment. During the training of our pre-trained weights, CIFAR-related classes have been excluded.

3.4   Dataset Selection

As described in Sect. 2, a common evaluation strategy tests the ability of the detector to discriminate between samples drawn from p_{in} and p_{out}^i. While this supervised evaluation approach is straightforward, the choice of the distributions against which the detector is tested is arbitrary and arguably often based more on convenience rather than theoretical considerations. As the performance of anomaly detection methods may fluctuate between different distributions, the choice of p_{in} and p_{out}^i may impact the inferential reproducibility. Furthermore, when training with outlier exposure, the choice of p_{out}^{train} can have a significant impact on the final performance: if the data distribution p_{out}^{train} is similar to the test outlier data distributions p_{out}^i, the model might be more likely to generalize between the train and test anomalies. Thus, the choice of the outlier dataset constitutes an important decision that is, to our knowledge, not well understood. Furthermore, when only the distributions of the datasets are defined (say, for example, the data follows a normal distribution), the sampling of the datasets itself can influence reproducibility.

Example. Figure 3 depicts the AUROC performance measure of several methods when tested to discriminate between samples from the training distribution p_{in} and different distributions p_{out}^i. As we can see, different methods yield different performance scores on different datasets.

Mitigation. When no reasonable assumptions on the anomalies can be made, a strategy to mitigate this performance variance is to test the system against various distributions.

MCHAD. To increase the finding reproducibility, we tested our method against anomalies from seven different distributions, covering synthetic and natural data.

3.5   Resource Limitations

The optimization of DNNs is a resource-intensive process. Extensive resource requirements limit the number of individuals that can reproduce a method. If the requirements are inherent to the proposed method and not caused by a particular implementation, they can also impact the reproducibility of results and findings.

Mitigation. To keep the groups of people that could potentially reproduce experiments as large as possible, the resource requirements should be reduced as much as possible. This can be achieved, for example, by using pre-trained models, which were also reported to increase the robustness of the models [7]. On the other hand, pre-trained weights can be seen as additional dependencies. Alternatively, results for models trained with less data or for fewer training iterations can be reported.

Example. We use feature encoders pre-trained on a downscaled version of the ImageNet, which decreases the number of epochs required until convergence (at $\approx 95\%$ accuracy) on the CIFAR-10 from 150 to 10.

MCHAD. Despite the reduced training time, our experiments take approximately 12 h on 21 A100 1g.5gb Multi-Instance GPUs in parallel.

3.6 Dependencies

While dependencies might be publicly available at the time of publication, this might change in the future. Introducing additional dependencies in the form of third-party software libraries, data, or pre-trained weights increases the chance that one or more dependencies required to run the experiments cease to be available, which can impede the reproducibility of a method.

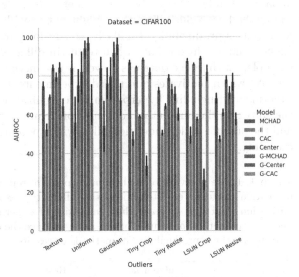

Fig. 3. Anomaly Detection performance of models on different OOD datasets over 21 training runs with error bars.

Example. The TinyImages database [19], which was often used as auxiliary data during optimization of anomaly detectors [4,8,13], has been recently taken down due to ethical concerns [1], which makes the reproduction of previous work based on this dataset impossible. Assuming that the rate r of dependencies being unavailable is identically and independently distributed, the probability that all dependencies are available after time t follows a binomial distribution and can be calculated as $(1-r)^{tn}$ where n is the number of dependencies. Assuming that each of the 212 software dependencies has a takedown rate of $r = 0.1\%$ per year, the probability that all of them will be available after ten years is $\approx 11.2\%$.

Mitigation. The most straightforward strategy is to reduce the number of dependencies. Furthermore, dependencies could be copied into the source code repository.

MCHAD. All dependencies, including code, data, and weights that were used, are documented and publicly available at the time of writing. As $\mathcal{D}_{train}^{out}$, we used a cleaned version of the TinyImages database provided by [8] with 300,000 images.

4   Complexity-Evidence Tradeoff

An overview of the different aspects of reproducibility, the corresponding mitigation strategies, and their relation to the different types of reproducibility is provided in Table 1. When comparing the different strategies, a trade-off becomes apparent: While less complex experiments are also easier to replicate in terms of the method reproducibility, they might not provide enough statistical evidence for results reproducibility. Similarly, conclusions drawn from a small number of experiments might not hold when tested in different experimental settings - for example, on different datasets - even if the method and the results are reproducible, which motivates additional experiments. On the other hand, extensive experiments (including hyperparameter optimization) increase the complexity of the software, the amount of computation required to conduct the experiments, and the number of dependencies, all of which potentially harm all types of reproducibility.

Table 1. Loose overview of challenging aspects of reproducibility with corresponding mitigation strategies used to address the different types of reproducibility. While some mitigation strategies increase the complexity of experiments to facilitate the reproducibility of method or results, others aim to reduce the complexity of the experiments to facilitate the reproducibility of methods or results.

Aspect	Inferential	Results	Method
Nondeterminism	More Experiments	More Experiments	
HP-Sensitivity	More Experiments		
Complexity		Decrease Complexity	Decrease Complexity
Dataset Selection	More Experiments		
Resource Limitations	Decrease Complexity	Decrease Complexity	Decrease Complexity
Dependencies			Reduce Dependencies

In our work, we focused on the strength of the obtained experimental evidence by comparing the performance of several methods and training with different random seeds on a large number of datasets. As a consequence, replicating our experiments requires significant computation and the availability of a large number of (transient) dependencies. Over time, it might become increasingly difficult to reproduce the exact numerical results we obtained since one or more dependencies (such as software libraries, datasets, or pre-trained weights) might be taken down. However, the extensive experiments improve the reproducibility of results and inferences.

In conclusion, we argue that the strength of the empirical evidence can be seen as more important than the reproducibility of the exact numerical results since knowledge gain - arguably the paramount goal of the scientific enterprise - is more likely to be robust when based on strong evidence, even if the exact numerical results in repeated experiments vary within the bounds of statistical uncertainty.

5 Conclusion

In this companion paper, we outlined and discussed several aspects of reproducibility often encountered in anomaly detection with deep neural networks. We documented a trade-off between the complexity of experiments, which decreases the reproducibility, and the strength of the empirical evidence obtained through them, which increases the reproducibility. Ultimately, we argued that the reproducibility of inferences through stronger evidence should be prioritized over the reproducibility of exact numerical results since the former contributes to the advancement of scientific knowledge.

References

1. Birhane, A., Prabhu, V.U.: Large image datasets: A pyrrhic win for computer vision? In: Proceedings of the IEEE/CVF Winter Conference on Applications of Computer Vision, pp. 1536–1546. IEEE (2021)
2. Bouthillier, X., Laurent, C., Vincent, P.: Unreproducible research is reproducible. In: International Conference on Machine Learning, pp. 725–734 (2019)
3. Chetlur, S., et al.: cuDNN: Efficient primitives for deep learning. arXiv preprint arXiv:1410.0759 (2014)
4. Dhamija, A.R., Günther, M., Boult, T.: Reducing network agnostophobia. In: Advances in Neural Information Processing Systems, pp. 9157–9168 (2018)
5. He, K., Zhang, X., Ren, S., Sun, J.: Deep residual learning for image recognition. In: Proceedings of the IEEE Conference on Computer Vision and Pattern Recognition, pp. 770–778 (2016)
6. Henderson, P., Islam, R., Bachman, P., Pineau, J., Precup, D., Meger, D.: Deep reinforcement learning that matters. In: Proceedings of the AAAI Conference on Artificial Intelligence, vol. 32 (2018)
7. Hendrycks, D., Lee, K., Mazeika, M.: Using pre-training can improve model robustness and uncertainty. In: International Conference on Machine Learning, pp. 2712–2721. PMLR (2019)
8. Hendrycks, D., Mazeika, M., Dietterich, T.: Deep anomaly detection with outlier exposure. In: International Conference on Learning Representations (2018)
9. Hutson, M.: Artificial intelligence faces reproducibility crisis. Science (2018)
10. Kirchheim, K., Filax, M., Ortmeier, F.: Multi-class hypersphere anomaly detection. In: Proceedings of the 26th International Conference for Pattern Recognition (August 2022)
11. Kirchheim, K., Filax, M., Ortmeier, F.: PyTorch-OOD: A library for out-of-distribution detection based on pytorch. In: Proceedings of the IEEE/CVF Conference on Computer Vision and Pattern Recognition (CVPR) Workshops, pp. 4351–4360 (June 2022)
12. Kirchheim, K., Gonschorek, T., Ortmeier, F.: Addressing randomness in evaluation protocols for out-of-distribution detection. In: 2nd Workshop on Artificial Intelligence for Anomalies and Novelties at IJCAI (2021)
13. Liu, W., Wang, X., Owens, J., Li, Y.: Energy-based out-of-distribution detection. In: Advances in Neural Information Processing Systems, vol. 33 (2020)
14. Lucic, M., Kurach, K., Michalski, M., Gelly, S., Bousquet, O.: Are GANs created equal? A large-scale study. In: Advances in Neural Information Processing Systems, pp. 700–709 (2018)

15. Nagarajan, P., Warnell, G., Stone, P.: The impact of nondeterminism on reproducibility in deep reinforcement learning. In: 2nd Reproducibility in Machine Learning Workshop at ICML (2018)
16. Ruff, L., et al.: A unifying review of deep and shallow anomaly detection. In: Proceedings of the IEEE (2021)
17. Russakovsky, O., et al.: Imagenet large scale visual recognition challenge. Int. J. Comput. Vision **115**(3), 211–252 (2015)
18. Summers, C., Dinneen, M.J.: Nondeterminism and instability in neural network optimization. In: International Conference on Machine Learning, pp. 9913–9922. PMLR (2021)
19. Torralba, A., Fergus, R., Freeman, W.T.: 80 million tiny images: a large data set for nonparametric object and scene recognition. IEEE Trans. Pattern Anal. Mach. Intell. **30**(11), 1958–1970 (2008)

On the Implementation of Baselines and Lightweight Conditional Model Extrapolation (LIMES) Under Class-Prior Shift

Paulina Tomaszewska[1]([✉])[iD] and Christoph H. Lampert[2][iD]

[1] Warsaw University of Technology, Faculty of Mathematics and Information Science, Warsaw, Poland
paulina.tomaszewska3.dokt@pw.edu.pl
[2] Institute of Science and Technology Austria (ISTA), Machine Learning and Computer Vision Group, Klosterneuburg, Austria

Abstract. This paper focuses on the implementation details of the baseline methods and a recent lightweight conditional model extrapolation algorithm *LIMES* [5] for streaming data under class-prior shift. *LIMES* achieves superior performance over the baseline methods, especially concerning the minimum-across-day accuracy, which is important for the users of the system. In this work, the key measures to facilitate reproducibility and enhance the credibility of the results are described.

Keywords: continual learning · non-stationary data · class-prior shift · reproducibility

1 Introduction

Offline Deep Learning solutions work well in production as long as the input at the prediction time has similar characteristics to the data used for training. Otherwise, if the discrepancy is substantial, the model may need to be updated by fine-tuning using new data. Another approach is to replace the previous model with a new one.

The relatively new paradigm is to train a model in a continuous manner on streaming data. However, in such a case, often the data drift problem arises. It may happen that at the production time, data from the new class occurs, features within the classes change or the class-prior shift happens. In the work, the latter issue is discussed mainly from the implementation standpoint. Following [5], *LIMES*, *incremental*, *random*, *ensemble* and *restart* algorithms are analyzed. The key aspects of the recently proposed *LIMES* method are adaptation at the training time (inspired by meta-learning solutions) and extrapolation of incoming data class distribution. The implementation of the methods is publicly available at github repository https://github.com/ptomaszewska/LIMES to facilitate the reproduction of the results.

B. Kerautret et al. (Eds.): RRPR 2022, LNCS 14068, pp. 67–73, 2023.
https://doi.org/10.1007/978-3-031-40773-4_6

2   Dataset

In Machine Learning, data is a starting point of any research. That is why this is so crucial to publicly share it (even in an anonymized manner) especially if the data is not artificially generated using the code [2,4]. Following this good practice, the exemplary `geo-location` dataset used in [5] to compare the performance of different methods, was planned to be shared in an original format. However, in the Terms of Service of the Twitter's free Streaming API[1], which was used for data collection, it is stated that it is not allowed to make large amounts of raw Twitter data available on the Web. In such a case, only the so-called *dehydrated* dataset was placed at the website[2] specified in the main paper. The dehydrated dataset means that json files with the text of tweets and metadata (downloaded using API) are compressed to only tweet ids. Later, the original dataset in a form of json files can be restored using *Twarc* tool[3]. To get started with the tool, the configuration needs to be done where the user has to provide Twitter application API keys and grant access to at least one Twitter account.

The process of restoring the tweets from their ids can be done with a single line of code: `twarc hydrate tweet_ids.txt > tweets_hydrated.jsonl`.
This process is called *rehydration*. The dehydrated dataset is stored on the website in two zip files, separately for each time subset: 1–5 days and 11–15 days. Each zip contains files in a format `geo-YYYY_MM_DD_HH.id` where tweet ids from one hour HH of a particular day YYYY-MM-DD are available. The size of each zip file is about 500 MB. However, please note that after rehydration, the size increases about 200 times.

3   Implementation

The source code available at the github repository[4] is under the Permissive MIT license (following the guidelines in [4]) which puts only very limited restrictions on reuse. While writing the implementation, we followed the good practices described in [4] like modularity - there are classes and functions with informative variable names to facilitate understanding. The repository contains python scripts for preprocessing of json files containing Twitter data, creating embeddings and implementation of the methods for the classification of data under class-prior shift. In addition, `requirements.txt` to facilitate the process of setting up the environment for the sake of experiments and the configuration scripts to run the experiments on SLURM queuing system[5] are provided. This is a step forward to the high level of reproducibility defined in [4]. Due to the large size of the dataset, it may be necessary to use a cluster for increased efficiency.

---

[1] https://developer.twitter.com/en/docs/tutorials/consuming-streaming-data.
[2] https://cvml.ist.ac.at/geo-tweets/.
[3] https://twarc-project.readthedocs.io/en/latest/.
[4] https://github.com/ptomaszewska/LIMES.
[5] https://slurm.schedmd.com/documentation.html.

3.1   Preprocessing of Raw Json Files with Twitter Data

After having the raw dataset downloaded, it should be processed to create files with a better-defined structure, making it easier for further use. The script `process_raw_data.py` is generic - it extracts more valuable information from metadata than is needed for the research. Information about the country from which the particular tweet originates is extracted based on longitude and latitude coordinates. For this purpose, the `countries.geojson` file is required, which can be downloaded from external repository[6]. Note that here the term country is considered in a broader sense following official codes in ISO 3166-1 where regions that are not independent but have their identity are treated as separate countries.

3.2   Embeddings

The next step in the algorithm is to use files generated in the previous stage to prepare input to the Machine Learning models. The jsonlines files are processed line by line. The two information sources are considered: tweet text and location given in a plain text where there is no control over the field content. Each of them is passed to the pretrained `distiluse-base-multilingual-cased-v1` multilingual sentence embedding network[7] (suitable for social media texts) to create embeddings. At this stage, the train/validation split with a ratio of 80:20 is performed at random. Later, the concatenated features from two sources are appended to the respective lists with training or validation samples. Later, at training time, the data source is decided on. When all the records from the json file (concerning data from one hour) are processed, the lists of features are saved to files with the `.npy` extension. This file extension ensures a binary format that results in a smaller file size and more efficient data loading. In the script for the generation of embeddings, the `country_codes.csv` file is used to decipher the code of the countries from the metadata. The file is provided in the repository. Later, the data stored in newly generated files is subsampled to create 10 data realizations (script `subsample_realizations.py`)

3.3   Machine Learning Models - Training and Evaluation

The implementation is written using *keras* framework with *tensorflow* backend. We prepared a custom training loop where the processing of streaming data is simulated - each sample is processed only once following the chronological order. To speed up the training process, the training step was wrapped using `tensorflow.function` decorator. The default mode in Tensoflow 2 is an eager execution which can slow down training but can be useful for debugging. Instead, by applying the decorator, global performance optimizations can be performed because the model is treated as a static graph.

---

[6] https://github.com/datasets/geo-countries/blob/master/data/countries.geojson.

[7] https://github.com/UKPLab/sentence-transformers.

The algorithms (*LIMES, incremental, random, ensemble* and *restart*) are ready to be used for the experiments on Twitter data to reproduce the results from the paper. However, the code is largely generic and can be adjusted to run the experiments on different datasets mainly by modifying the dimensionality of the expected input and output of the respective layers.

The pseudocode for the five methods is described in Algorithm 1. Note that in the case of *incremental*, the model is trained in a continuous manner without any modification that could be applied if any of the conditions specified in lines 7–13 is met. In order to implement a non-trainable bias correction term in a fully connected layer, a custom class was defined.

Algorithm 1. A generic training algorithm

1: $data\_source \leftarrow \{tweet, location, tweet + location\}$
2: $p \leftarrow U(0, 250)$
3: initiate model or models (collection of 24 models in case of *ensemble*)
4: **for** $counter \leftarrow 0$ to all_hours **do**
5:     **if** $counter > 0$ **then**
6:         $X\_val, y\_val \leftarrow load\_data(filenames\_val, counter)$
7:         **if** $LIMES$ **then**
8:             $p\_future \leftarrow extrapolation(all\_historical\_p)$
9:             $model \leftarrow model(p\_future)$ ▷ apply bias correction term
10:         **else if** $random$ **then**
11:             $p\_future \leftarrow random(all\_historical\_p)$
12:             $model \leftarrow model(p\_future)$ ▷ apply bias correction term
13:         **else if** $ensemble$ **then**
14:             $model \leftarrow models[counter]$
15:         **end if**
16:         $accuracy = validation(X\_val, y\_val, model)$
17:         **if** $restart$ **then**
18:             initiate $model$
19:         **end if**
20:     **end if**
21:     $X\_train, y\_train \leftarrow load\_data(filenames\_train, counter)$
22:     $y\_pred \leftarrow model(X\_train, y\_train)$
23:     $loss \leftarrow CrossEntropy(y\_pred, y)$
24:     update model weights
25: **end for**

To reproduce the paper results, it is recommended to run experiments with different combinations of parameters (subset, realization, data source, model).

3.4 Running Experiments Efficiently

Each of the steps (preprocessing, embedding generation, training) can be run with different parameters in an automated way using bash scripts provided at the repository. One of those is `run_process_raw_data.sh` which is used to call a python script for data preprocessing iterating over different files. In an analogous way, the python script to create text embeddings can be executed. Running training of Machine Learning methods can be done efficiently using two bash scripts from the repository (`run_sbatch.sh` and `run_training.sh`). In the first one, the loops iterating over different parameters of experiments are defined. In the loops, the `run_training.sh` script is run that sends a task execution to the SLURM queue.

4   Reproducibility

The experimental process should be repeatable and produce consistent results and conclusions [3]. Therefore, in the source code, the random seed was set at different stages of the pipeline: when creating a training/validation split and training of the Machine Learning model (especially important for weight initialization). To facilitate the reproduction, detailed instructions on how to get the dataset and run the code are provided together with the comments in the scripts. Not only can the results of the experiments be reproduced but also the figures presented in the paper because the appropriate script is available at the repository.

To facilitate the reproduction of the results described in papers, authors sometimes provide Google Colaboratory notebooks. In our case, it is not done for several reasons. First of all, the data cannot be publicly shared in its original form, instead, it is placed online in dehydrated form that requires the process of rehydration where the configuration step is needed. It involves creating an account on Twitter application API and providing personal keys to configure the *Twarc* tool. Moreover, the dataset is of significant size; therefore, it could not be directly stored within the Google Colaboratory session. Lastly, the computations take significant time so it may be better to run it on the cluster if possible.

5   Credibility of Results

As stated in [1,3], the common problems with credibility originate in selective reporting and overclaiming of the results, by drawing conclusions that go beyond the evidence presented (e.g. due to an insufficient number of experiments). We have taken measures to eliminate these problems.

We generated many dataset subsets - 10 different realizations of data for 2 different time subsets (*"early"* and *"late"*) using 3 different data sources (*"tweet"*, *"location"* and concatenation of both). The motivation behind analyzing different data sources was to investigate whether there is a correlation between the task difficulty and the performance boost of the proposed method.

In order to reduce bias that could be introduced by the choice of the metric and show a broader spectrum of advantages and limitations of *LIMES*, two different metrics are computed - average per-day accuracy and minimum-across-day accuracy (in both cases mean and standard deviations are reported). The exact way in which the metrics are computed is provided in the code. It turns out that in the case of minimum-across-day accuracy, the *LIMES*'s boost of performance is higher than in the case of average per-day accuracy. To account for the random nature of the experimental results, we applied the Wilcoxon statistical test to validate the performance of *LIMES* over the *incremental* baseline method which reaches the closest results to *LIMES*. Such an analysis is combined with the results visualization. The plots with the results obtained using the aforementioned methods to enhance credibility are shown in Fig. 1.

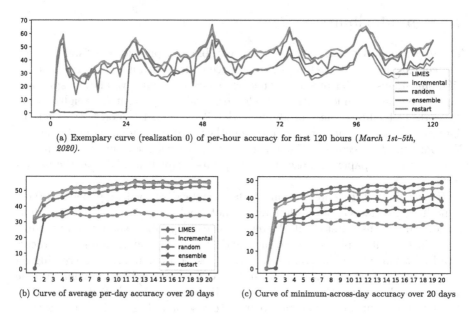

(a) Exemplary curve (realization 0) of per-hour accuracy for first 120 hours (*March 1st–5th, 2020*).

(b) Curve of average per-day accuracy over 20 days

(c) Curve of minimum-across-day accuracy over 20 days

Fig. 1. Classifier accuracy over time for the proposed *LIMES* and baseline methods in one of the tested settings (*tweet* features, subset *early*).

Note that the parameters of the models were left at default values. It may be possible that doing a careful hyperparameter search could improve the model performance.

6   Conclusions

We prepared a repository with the implementation of baseline methods and *LIMES* dealing with class-prior shift. To answer the need for reproducibility and reliability of results, the following (among others) measures were taken: (1) we provided detailed information on how to recreate the dataset used in the paper, (2) made the source code publicly available, (3) paid attention to setting the random seed, (4) created many different variants of the datasets and (5) applied the statistical test to verify the statistical significance of the achieved performance gain. We believe that this repository can be valuable for other researchers working on the topic of modelling streaming data under class-prior shift. Hopefully, it would fasten their work by using already implemented baselines.

References

1. Baker, M.: 1,500 scientists lift the lid on reproducibility. Nature **533**, 452–454 (2016). https://doi.org/10.1038/533452a
2. Liu, C., Gao, C., Xia, X., Lo, D., Grundy, J., Yang, X.: On the reproducibility and replicability of deep learning in software engineering. ACM Trans. Softw. Eng. Methodol. **31**(1), 1–46 (2022). https://doi.org/10.1145/3477535
3. Pineau, J., et al.: Improving reproducibility in machine learning research (a report from the NeurIPS 2019 reproducibility program). J. Mach. Learn. Res. **22**(164), 1–20 (2021). http://jmlr.org/papers/v22/20-303.html
4. Tatman, R., Vanderplas, J., Dane, S.: A practical taxonomy of reproducibility for machine learning research. In: Reproducibility in Machine Learning - Workshop at ICML (2018)
5. Tomaszewska, P., Lampert, C.H.: Lightweight conditional model extrapolation for streaming data under class-prior shift. In: 26th International Conference on Pattern Recognition (2022)

Special Reproducibility Track
from DGMM Event

Combining Max-Tree and CNN for Segmentation of Cellular FIB-SEM Images

Cyril Meyer[1]([✉]) [iD], Étienne Baudrier[1] [iD], Patrick Schultz[2] [iD], and Benoît Naegel[1] [iD]

[1] ICube, UMR 7357 CNRS, Université de Strasbourg, Strasbourg, France
cymeyer@unistra.fr
[2] IGBMC, UMR 7104 CNRS, U1258 INSERM, Université de Strasbourg, Strasbourg, France

Abstract. Max-tree (or component-tree) is a hierarchical representation which associates to a scalar image a descriptive data structure induced by the inclusion relation between the binary components obtained at successive level-sets. Various attributes related to these binary components can be computed and stored into the tree.

Max-trees have been involved in many applications, enabling to perform attribute filtering in an efficient algorithmic way. Since the resulting images do not contain any new contour, these kind of filters are called *connected operators*.

In this paper, we propose to rely on max-trees and attribute filters to enrich the input of a convolutional neural network (CNN) to improve a task of segmentation. More precisely, two approaches are considered: a first approach in which images are preprocessed using attribute filters and a second approach in which maps of attributes relying on max-trees are computed. Based on these two different approaches, the resulting maps are used as additional input in a standard CNN in a context of semantic segmentation.

We propose to compare different attributes and nodes selection strategies and to experiment their usage on a practical problem: the segmentation of the mitochondria and endoplasmic-reticulum in Focused Ion Beam milling combined with Scanning Electron Microscopy (FIB-SEM) images.

We provide original images, annotations, source code and a documentation to reproduce the experimentation results.

Keywords: Mathematical Morphology · Connected Operators · Max-tree · Segmentation · Deep Learning · Convolutional Neural Network · Electron Microscopy · FIB-SEM

1 Introduction

The max-tree structure [16,21] allows to perform efficiently attribute filtering [7] and has been involved in many image processing applications. The resulting operators are called *connected* [22] since they do not create new contours nor modify

IdEx Doctoral contract, Université de Strasbourg.

their position. In [3], Farfan *et al.* have suggested that max-tree attributes could be used to feed a deep convolutional neural network (CNN) in order to improve the results of detection and segmentation tasks. Following and generalizing this approach, the aim of this paper is to provide a reproducible framework enabling to perform various experiments involving max-trees and CNN in a context of semantic segmentation of cellular FIB-SEM images.

Our contributions are twofold: in a first approach, input images are preprocessed using various attribute filters [12] and then concatenated as additional inputs of a CNN. In a second approach, maps of attributes are computed from the max-tree and then added in a CNN, following Farfan *et al.* approach.

Finally, our work aims to be handy. For this purpose, all the methods we propose can be used on a high-end workstation and do not require large GPU/TPU clusters. Also, our source code, datasets (original images, annotations) and documentation are publicly available, allowing everybody to reproduce the results, but also to reuse the code for their own needs.

2 State of the Art

To address the segmentation of cellular electron microscopy images, the state-of-the-art methods are currently based on CNN [2,5,9,12,18,19,24] and the U-Net architecture remains mainly used. However, despite the good accuracy that can be obtained using these methods, the resulting segmentations can still suffer from various imperfections. In particular, thin and elongated objects such as endoplasmic reticulum can be disconnected and some parts may be distorted [12]. These effects may be the result of the context window that is fixed and too narrow in the first layer of the CNN, preventing to capture sufficient global information.

To overcome this, Farfan *et al.* [3] have proposed to enrich a CNN with attributes computed from the max-tree, enabling to capture at a pixel level, an information that may be non-local.

In the sequel of this paper, we will explore various strategies in order to incorporate max-tree attributes into CNN with the aim of potentially improving segmentation results.

3 Methods

3.1 Max-Tree

Let $I : E \rightarrow V$ be a discrete, scalar (i.e. grayscale) image, with $E \subseteq \mathbb{Z}^n$ and $V \subseteq \mathbb{Z}$. A cut of I at level v is defined as: $X_v(I) = \{p \in E | I(p) \geq v\}$. Let $C[X]$ be the set of connected components of X. Let Ψ be the set of all the connected components of the cuts of I:

$$\Psi(I) = \bigcup_{v \in V} \{C[X_v(I)]\}$$

The relation $\subseteq$ is a partial order on Ψ. The transitive reduction of the relation $\subseteq$ on Ψ induces a graph called the Hasse diagram of $(\Psi, \subseteq)$. This graph is a tree, the root of which is E. The rooted tree $\mathcal{T} = (\Psi, L, E)$ is called the max-tree of I, with Ψ, L, E being respectively the set of nodes, the set of edges and the root of $\mathcal{T}$. The parent node of N, denoted $Par(N)$, is the unique node such that: $(Par(N), N) \in L$ and $N \subseteq Par(N)$ for $N \neq E$. The *branch* associated to a node is the set of its ancestors and is defined for a node $N \in \Psi$ by: $Br(N) = \{X \in \Psi \mid X \supseteq N\}$.

In this work, the computation of the max-tree is based on the recursive implementation of Salembier [21], and node attributes are computed during the construction of the tree. In the rest of this paper, we will focus on the following attributes which have been proposed in the literature:

- The height H is the minimum gray level of the connected component [21].
- The area A is the number of pixels in the connected component [21].
- The contour length CT represents the number of pixels that have both a neighbor inside and outside the component [20].
- The contrast C is the difference between the maximum and minimum grey-level in the connected component [21].
- The complexity CPL represents the contour length CT divided by the area A [20].
- The compacity (sometimes named compactness or circularity) CPA is the area A divided by the square of the contour length CT^2 [22].
- The volume V is the sum of the difference between the pixels values in the node and the node height [16].
- The mean gradient border MGB represents the mean value of the gradient magnitude for the contour pixels of the component [3].

The tree attributes can be merged in order to compute an image, by associating to each pixel an attribute value computed from its corresponding nodes [3]. Each pixel p belongs to several nodes: the connected component N including p in the level-set $X_{I(p)}(I)$ and all the nodes belonging to its *branch* $Br(N)$. To associate a unique value to each pixel, different policies can be implemented: for example, by keeping the maximum, the minimum or the mean value of the attributes of the branch nodes [3].

In this work, we propose the following strategy. For each pixel p, the set of nodes belonging to the branch of p is retrieved, and only a subset of nodes having an attribute value in a certain range (given as a parameter) is kept. From this set, the node N_{best} optimizing a certain stability criterion is kept. Finally, the value of p in the resulting image is set to the attribute value of N_{best}. The resulting image is normalized in the range $V = [\![0, 255]\!]$.

The criterion used to retrieve the optimal node is based on the concept of Maximally Stable Extremal Regions proposed by Matas *et al.* [10]. The idea is to retrieve the most stable regions based on the area variation between successive nodes since these regions represent salient objects of the image. For each node $N \in \Psi$, with $N \neq E$ (i.e. different from the root), we define two stability attributes as follows:

$$\nabla_A(N) = \frac{\mid A(Par(N)) - A(N) \mid}{\mid H(Par(N)) - H(N) \mid} \cdot \frac{1}{A(N)}$$

$$\Delta_A(N) = \mid \nabla_A(Par(N)) - \nabla_A(N) \mid$$

where $Par(N)$ defines the parent node of N.

3.2 Segmentation

We base our segmentation method on fully convolutional networks for semantic segmentation. We use attribute filtered images or max-tree attribute maps as additional input of our network. We feed the network with the original and the preprocessed images, concatenating them in the color (spectral) channels.

For model architectures, we use a 2D U-Net [19], which is a reference for biomedical image segmentation. A 3D U-Net [2] could also be used, but the results are not necessarily better [17,23,25] and the computational cost of training the model is much higher. In a preliminary experiment, we have compared 2D and 3D models, using an equal number of parameters and same input size and the 2D U-Net performs as well, if not better than the 3D one.

Each block of the network is composed of convolutions with ReLU activation, followed by batch normalization [6] and a residual connection [4], see Fig. 1. We use a 50% dropout entering the deepest block to avoid over fitting. We always use padded convolution to maintain the spatial dimension of the output. The model starts with 64 filters at the first level, for a total of 32.4 millions parameters.

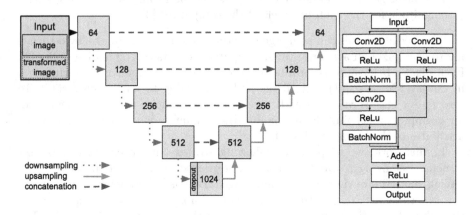

Fig. 1. U-Net architecture and its backbone block. The number in the box corresponds to the number of filters at this level for the convolutions blocks. The network is fed with the original and the preprocessed images, concatenating them in the color channels.

We train our models by minimizing the Dice loss. For the binary segmentation task, we use classical Dice loss and for multi-class segmentation problems, we use a weighted mean of the loss for each class, with the same weight ($W = 0.5$) for our two classes. We note X the ground truth, Y the prediction, W the weight list and C the class list. The ε term is used for stability when $\sum (X + Y) = 0$ and is set to 10^{-4}.

$$L_{Dice}(X,Y) = 1 - \frac{2 \cdot \sum X \cdot Y + \varepsilon}{\sum (X + Y) + \varepsilon}$$

$$L_{DiceMean}(X,Y,W) = \frac{1}{|C|} \sum_{c \in C} W_c \cdot L_{Dice}(X_c, Y_c)$$

The model is trained for 128 epochs, each epoch is composed of 512 batches, a batch is composed of 8 patches and a patch is a $256 \times 256 \times C$ subpart of the image, with C the number of channels. We use random 90° rotation, horizontal and vertical flips for data augmentation on the patches. We trained our model using Adam [8] optimizer with the following parameters: $\alpha = 0.001$, $\beta_1 = 0.9$, $\beta_2 = 0.999$, $\varepsilon = 1e{-}07$.

3.3   Evaluation Metrics

To evaluate our models, we binarize the model prediction with a threshold at 0.5. To predict a slice, we use the whole slice to avoid the negative border effects of padding.

To evaluate our results, we use the F1-Score which is a region-based metric, and the average symmetric surface distance (ASSD) which is a boundary-based metrics. In fact, the F1-Score is equivalent to the Dice Score. We note respectively TP, FP and FN the cardinal of the sets of true positives, false positives and false negatives. X is the ground truth, Y the binary prediction and ∂X the boundary of X.

$$\text{F1-Score} = \frac{2 \times TP}{2 \times TP + FP + FN}$$

$$\text{ASSD}(X,Y) = \frac{\sum_{x \in \partial X} d(x,Y) + \sum_{y \in \partial Y} d(y,X)}{|\partial X| + |\partial Y|}$$

with $d(x,A) = \min_{y \in A} \|x - y\|_2$.

4   Experiments

In this section, we test the improvement of the segmentation thanks to the addition of filtered images in the input. We compare the original image input with the enriched version. We also compare in the same time a multi-class segmentation model and two binary segmentations models. Finally, we repeat each of these configurations 11 times. In total, 363 models have been trained for this experiment, each training lasts about 5 h with an NVIDIA GeForce RTX 2080 Ti.

First, we define the filters we use as our experiment variable. Attributes are selected for their potential help for the segmentation, we list the selected filters in Table 1 (attribute maps strategy) and 2 (connected operators strategy), and renamed them for sake of simplicity.

Table 1. List of used attribute maps filters and their names.

Name	Attribute	Criterion	Limit
Contrast$_{\Delta_A}$	C	Δ_A	$0 \leq A \leq 1024^2$
Complexity$_{\Delta_A}$	CPL	Δ_A	$0 \leq A \leq 1024^2$
Compacity$_{\Delta_A}$	CPA	Δ_A	$CPA \leq 50$
Volume$_{\Delta_A}$	V	Δ_A	$0 \leq A \leq 1024^2$
MGB	MGB	MGB	$0 \leq A \leq 1024^2$

Table 2. List of used connected filters and their names. The "inverse" column is checked when filter is applied on the inverted image.

Name	Attribute	Range	Inverse
Contrast α	C	$[10, 150]$	
Contrast β	C	$[10, 150]$	✓
Area α	A	$[2 \times 32^2, 1024^2]$	
Area β	A	$[64^2, +\infty]$	
Area γ	A	$[16^2, 512^2]$	✓

Before processing the image with a max-tree, we apply a low pass filter (9×9 mean filter).

4.1 Data

We perform our experimentation on a stack of 80 slices from a 3D FIB-SEM image. Each slice has a size of 1536×1408. The image represents a HeLa cell and has an $(x \times y \times z)$ resolution of $5\,\mathrm{nm} \times 5\,\mathrm{nm} \times 20\,\mathrm{nm}$. A ground truth is available on the stack for two kinds of organelles (i.e. cell subunits) : mito-chondria and endoplasmic reticulum. A default background class is affected to non-assigned pixel. An example slice with label is available in Figs. 3 and 4 in Sect. A.2. Figures 5 to 14 depict the slice for each applied filter.

We divide the stack into 3 sets: training (first 40 slices), validation (next 20 slices) and test (last 20 slices). The training set is used to train the network, the validation set to select the best model during the training and the test set to provide evaluation metrics.

4.2   Results

Figs. 2a and 2b depict the F1-score on the two classes of segmentation as box plots. Detailed mean and variation score are available in Table 3 and 4 in Sect. A.1.

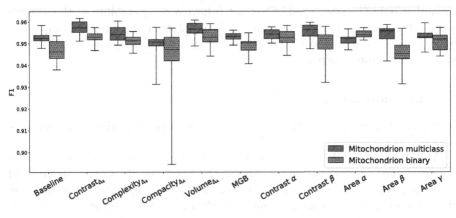

(a) F1-score on mitochondria.

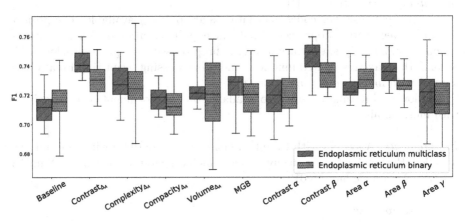

(b) F1-score on endoplasmic reticulum.

Fig. 2. The box shows the quartiles of the results, while the whiskers extend to show the rest of the distribution.

Baseline Segmentation Results. Mitochondria are well segmented with a median F1-score up to 95% in multi-class segmentation and 94% in binary segmentation, which let a little possible improvement. Median F1-scores for reticulum up to 72% and 71% in multi-class and binary segmentation respectively. This thin organelle is indeed more difficult to segment.

Additional-input segmentation results On the mitochondria, the additional inputs improve the results for 11 cases out of 20 and 17 out of 20 for the reticulum. The gain on the reticulum is very interesting since it is the more difficult to segment for the baseline setup. The following additional inputs improve the result in all the four tests (binary and multi-class segmentations on mitochondria and reticulum): $Contrast_{\Delta_A}$, $Complexity_{\Delta_A}$, Contrast β. Moreover, the whiskers show that only $Contrast_{\Delta_A}$ and Contrast β have a good stability in this experiment. These two inputs are therefore good candidates to be additional inputs to improve segmentation results. On the contrary, $Compacity_{\Delta_A}$ and MGB do not yield to any improvement.

4.3   Reproducibility

In this section, we present the required steps to reproduce the results we presented.

We follow the ACM definition of reproducibility: *"The measurement can be obtained with stated precision by a different team using the same measurement procedure, the same measuring system, under the same operating conditions, in the same or a different location on multiple trials. For computational experiments, this means that an independent group can obtain the same result using the author's own artifacts."* [1]

For this purpose, our codes and datasets are publicly available. The project is split between three subprojects. First, the experimentation detailed documentation, training scripts, evaluation scripts, preprocessing script, results logs [11]. Second, the max-tree related functions and preprocessing script [14]. Finally, the dataset with images and annotations [13]

The following information are also available on the documentation repository with more details.

Requirements. A system with Ubuntu 18.04.6 (or compatible) with g++ and git installed. Python 3.6.9 with an environment including TensorFlow 2.6.2, NumPy, SciPy, scikit-image and MedPy.

Image preprocessing

- Prepare data for extraction with low pass filter.
  ```
  python 01_mean_filter.py
  ```
- Extract attribute image from pre-processed images.
  ```
  ./build_bin_requirements.sh
  ./02_attribute_image.sh
  ```
- Crop the image to the annotated area and construct a tiff stack.
  ```
  python 03_crop_roi.py
  ```

Network Training and Evaluation. For the following commands, `$ID` is a unique identifier for the train, `$INPUT` is the folder containing the dataset, `$OUTPUT` is the folder containing the trained models and evaluation metrics, `$DATASET` select the dataset to use (in our case, binary or multi-class dataset), $SETUP select the experiment to run. An automation bash script is available on the repository to run all the 33 setups once.

- Train the networks
  ```
  python train.py $ID $INPUT $OUTPUT $DATASET $SETUP
  ```
- Evaluate the networks
  ```
  python eval.py $ID $INPUT $OUTPUT $DATASET $SETUP BEST
  ```

Result Analysis and Figures Reproduction. Since the output of each model evaluation is a comma separated values (CSV) file, the analysis of the results can be done using various tools. We propose to use a Jupyter notebook with Pandas and Seaborn, merging the CSV files into a single dataframe. An example analysis.ipynb notebook is provided on the GitHub, which we use to produce our result figures and tables.

5   Conclusion

In this paper, we have presented a detailed experimental setup to evaluate the use of additional input in a CNN based segmentation task. The additional inputs are attribute maps obtained from a max-tree representation of the image. The evaluation is made on segmentation tasks in the context of 3D electronic microscopy. If most of the additional inputs improve one segmentation task, two of them – namely Contrast$_{\Delta_A}$ and Contrast β– improve all the tested segmentation tasks in terms of median F1-score and stability. Further than the segmentation results, the setup inspired from [3] has been entirely implemented in C++ and Python and is proposed in open access to make it reproducible.

As a perspective of this work, the feature extraction method based on max-tree attributes presented in this paper could be used for other applications. For example, it would be interesting to compute the max-tree directly inside the model and to use the attributes images as a nonlinear filter. Also, the attribute maps could be used as feature maps for more simple and explainable classifier as random forests or even decision tree. Besides, the Δ_A attributes we defined could be used in an interactive segmentation setup, where a single pixel will allow to select an interesting node, selecting an object connected component over a background. Finally, we proposed here a max-tree based method, but an extension to the tree of shapes [15] could be interesting and add more information to the image.

Acknowledgements. We acknowledge the High Performance Computing Center of the University of Strasbourg for supporting this work by providing scientific support and access to computing resources. Part of the computing resources were funded by the Equipex Equip@Meso project (Programme Investissements d'Avenir) and the CPER Alsacalcul/Big Data. We thank D. Spehner from the Institut de Génétique et de Biologie Moléculaire et Cellulaire for providing the images and V. Mallouh for providing the annotations. We acknowledge the use of resources of the French Infrastructure for Integrated Structural Biology FRISBI ANR-10-INBS-05 and of Instruct-ERIC. We acknowledge that this work is supported by an IdEx doctoral contract, Université de Strasbourg.

A   Appendix

A.1   Results

In the following tables, the mean and deviation are computed over the 8 best model out of 11, selected using the F1-score on the validation set.

Table 3. F1 score and ASSD for mitochondria segmentation

Setup	Binary		Multi-class	
	F1	ASSD	F1	ASSD
Baseline	0.949 ±0.004	3.742 ±1.970	0.952 ±0.003	5.761 ±5.315
Contrast$_{\Delta_A}$	**0.953** ±0.002	**1.208** ±0.616	**0.958** ±0.003	1.531 ±0.490
Complexity$_{\Delta_A}$	0.951 ±0.003	1.559 ±0.647	0.956 ±0.003	**1.211** ±0.384
Compacity$_{\Delta_A}$	0.949 ±0.006	2.495 ±3.027	0.951 ±0.001	2.786 ±2.305
Volume$_{\Delta_A}$	**0.954** ±0.003	1.226 ±0.260	**0.957** ±0.003	**1.280** ±0.370
MGB	0.950 ±0.003	2.124 ±0.996	0.953 ±0.002	1.654 ±0.345
Contrast α	**0.954** ±0.004	**1.007** ±0.274	0.955 ±0.002	1.639 ±0.932
Contrast β	0.951 ±0.006	1.797 ±0.873	**0.957** ±0.003	1.698 ±1.301
Area α	**0.954** ±0.002	1.499 ±0.839	0.952 ±0.003	1.950 ±0.916
Area β	0.948 ±0.005	2.459 ±2.478	0.955 ±0.002	1.711 ±0.492
Area γ	0.952 ±0.003	1.244 ±0.318	0.954 ±0.004	2.639 ±3.522

Table 4. F1 score and ASSD for endoplasmic reticulum segmentation

Setup	Binary		Multi-class	
	F1	ASSD	F1	ASSD
Baseline	0.721 ±0.013	7.758 ±0.740	0.718 ±0.013	8.282 ±1.037
Contrast$_{\Delta_A}$	0.738 ±0.009	7.767 ±0.877	**0.747** ±0.011	7.903 ±0.425
Complexity$_{\Delta_A}$	**0.741** ±0.015	7.720 ±0.689	0.735 ±0.011	**7.232** ±0.817
Compacity$_{\Delta_A}$	0.721 ±0.014	8.810 ±1.012	0.725 ±0.008	8.535 ±0.691
Volume$_{\Delta_A}$	**0.744** ±0.011	7.522 ±0.494	0.732 ±0.011	7.817 ±0.828
MGB	0.729 ±0.013	8.526 ±0.646	0.729 ±0.009	8.614 ±0.468
Contrast α	0.736 ±0.012	8.910 ±0.680	0.728 ±0.013	8.327 ±0.783
Contrast β	**0.741** ±0.016	7.715 ±0.520	**0.748** ±0.007	7.407 ±0.784
Area α	0.734 ±0.009	**6.414** ±0.677	0.728 ±0.011	7.448 ±1.507
Area β	0.733 ±0.006	8.296 ±1.494	0.741 ±0.007	7.862 ±0.901
Area γ	0.733 ±0.009	8.243 ±0.584	0.729 ±0.014	8.693 ±0.518

A.2   Example Preprocessing Visualization

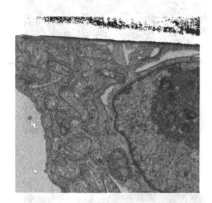

Fig. 3. Original image

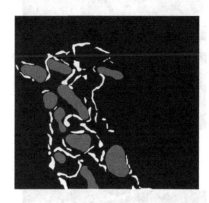

Fig. 4. Label, mitochondria in gray, endoplasmic reticulum in white

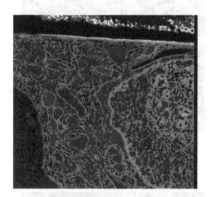

Fig. 5. Contrast$_{\Delta_A}$

Fig. 6. Complexity$_{\Delta_A}$

Fig. 7. Compacity$_{\Delta_A}$

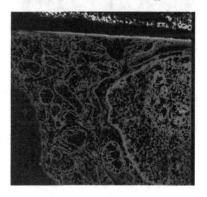

Fig. 8. Volume$_{\Delta_A}$

Fig. 9. MGB

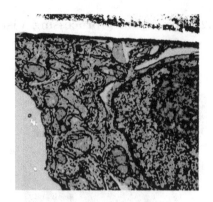

Fig. 10. Contrast α

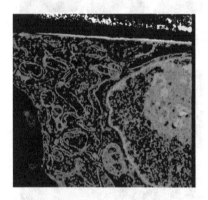

Fig. 11. Contrast β

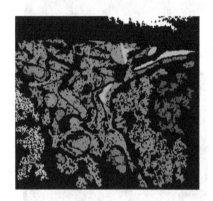

Fig. 12. Area α

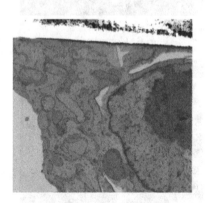

Fig. 13. Area β

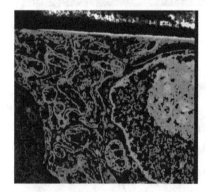

Fig. 14. Area γ

References

1. ACM: Artifact Review and Badging - vol 1.1. https://www.acm.org/publications/policies/artifact-review-and-badging-current
2. Çiçek, Ö., Abdulkadir, A., Lienkamp, S.S., Brox, T., Ronneberger, O.: 3D U-Net: Learning Dense Volumetric Segmentation from Sparse Annotation. In: Ourselin, S., Joskowicz, L., Sabuncu, M.R., Unal, G., Wells, W. (eds.) Medical Image Computing and Computer-Assisted Intervention – MICCAI 2016, pp. 424–432. Lecture Notes in Computer Science, Springer International Publishing, Cham (2016). https://doi.org/10.1007/978-3-319-46723-8_49
3. Farfan Cabrera, D.L., Gogin, N., Morland, D., Naegel, B., Papathanassiou, D., Passat, N.: Segmentation of Axillary and Supraclavicular Tumoral Lymph Nodes in PET/CT: A Hybrid CNN/Component-Tree Approach. In: 2020 25th International Conference on Pattern Recognition (ICPR), pp. 6672–6679 (Jan 2021). https://doi.org/10.1109/ICPR48806.2021.9412343
4. He, K., Zhang, X., Ren, S., Sun, J.: Deep Residual Learning for Image Recognition. In: 2016 IEEE Conference on Computer Vision and Pattern Recognition (CVPR), pp. 770–778. IEEE, Las Vegas, NV, USA (2016). https://doi.org/10.1109/CVPR.2016.90
5. Heinrich, L., et al.: Whole-cell organelle segmentation in volume electron microscopy. Nature pp. 1–6 (2021). https://doi.org/10.1038/s41586-021-03977-3
6. Ioffe, S., Szegedy, C.: Batch Normalization: Accelerating Deep Network Training by Reducing Internal Covariate Shift. In: Proceedings of the 32nd International Conference on Machine Learning, pp. 448–456. PMLR (2015)
7. Jones, R.: Connected filtering and segmentation using component trees. Comput. Vis. Image Underst. **75**(3), 215–228 (1999). https://doi.org/10.1006/cviu.1999.0777
8. Kingma, D.P., Ba, J.: Adam: A Method for Stochastic Optimization. In: Bengio, Y., LeCun, Y. (eds.) 3rd International Conference on Learning Representations, ICLR 2015, San Diego, CA, USA, May 7–9, 2015, Conference Track Proceedings (2015)
9. Liu, J., et al.: Automatic reconstruction of mitochondria and endoplasmic reticulum in electron microscopy volumes by deep learning. Front. Neurosci. 14 (2020). https://doi.org/10.3389/fnins.2020.00599
10. Matas, J., Chum, O., Urban, M., Pajdla, T.: Robust wide-baseline stereo from maximally stable extremal regions. Image Vis. Comput. **22**(10), 761–767 (2004). https://doi.org/10.1016/j.imavis.2004.02.006
11. Meyer, C.: CTAISegmentationCNN. GitHub repository (2022). https://github.com/Cyril-Meyer/DGMM2022-RRPR-CTAISegmentationCNN
12. Meyer, C., Mallouh, V., Spehner, D., Baudrier, É., Schultz, P., Naegel, B.: Automatic Multi Class Organelle Segmentation For Cellular Fib-Sem Images. In: 2021 IEEE 18th International Symposium on Biomedical Imaging (ISBI), pp. 668–672 (2021). https://doi.org/10.1109/ISBI48211.2021.9434075
13. Meyer, C., Mallouh, V., Spehner, D., Schultz, P.: DGMM2022-RRPR-MEYER-DATA. GitHub repository (2022). https://github.com/Cyril-Meyer/DGMM2022-RRPR-MEYER-DATA
14. Meyer, C., Naegel, B.: ComponentTreeAttributeImage. GitHub repository (2022). https://github.com/Cyril-Meyer/DGMM2022-RRPR-ComponentTreeAttributeImage

15. Monasse, P., Guichard, F.: Fast computation of a contrast-invariant image representation. IEEE Trans. Image Process. **9**(5), 860–872 (2000). https://doi.org/10.1109/83.841532

16. Najman, L., Couprie, M.: Building the component tree in quasi-linear time. IEEE Trans. Image Process. **15**(11), 3531–3539 (2006). https://doi.org/10.1109/TIP.2006.877518

17. Nemoto, T., et al.: Efficacy evaluation of 2D, 3D U-Net semantic segmentation and atlas-based segmentation of normal lungs excluding the trachea and main bronchi. J. Radiat. Res. **61**(2), 257–264 (2020). https://doi.org/10.1093/jrr/rrz086

18. Oztel, I., Yolcu, G., Ersoy, I., White, T., Bunyak, F.: Mitochondria segmentation in electron microscopy volumes using deep convolutional neural network. In: 2017 IEEE International Conference on Bioinformatics and Biomedicine (BIBM), pp. 1195–1200 (2017). https://doi.org/10.1109/BIBM.2017.8217827

19. Ronneberger, O., Fischer, P., Brox, T.: U-Net: Convolutional Networks for Biomedical Image Segmentation. In: Navab, N., Hornegger, J., Wells, W.M., Frangi, A.F. (eds.) Medical Image Computing and Computer-Assisted Intervention – MICCAI 2015, pp. 234–241. Lecture Notes in Computer Science, Springer International Publishing, Cham (2015). https://doi.org/10.1007/978-3-319-24574-4_28

20. Salembier, P., Brigger, P., Casas, J., Pardas, M.: Morphological operators for image and video compression. IEEE Trans. Image Process. **5**(6), 881–898 (1996). https://doi.org/10.1109/83.503906

21. Salembier, P., Oliveras, A., Garrido, L.: Antiextensive connected operators for image and sequence processing. IEEE Trans. Image Process. **7**(4), 555–570 (1998). https://doi.org/10.1109/83.663500

22. Salembier, P., Wilkinson, M.H.: Connected operators. IEEE Signal Process. Mag. **26**(6), 136–157 (2009). https://doi.org/10.1109/MSP.2009.934154

23. Srikrishna, M., et al.: Comparison of two-dimensional- and three-dimensional-based u-net architectures for brain tissue classification in one-dimensional brain CT. front. Comput. Neurosci. **15**, 785244 (2022)

24. Xiao, C., et al.: Automatic mitochondria segmentation for EM data using a 3D supervised convolutional network. Front. Neuroanat. **12** (2018). https://doi.org/10.3389/fnana.2018.00092

25. Zettler, N., Mastmeyer, A.: Comparison of 2D vs. 3D Unet Organ Segmentation in abdominal 3D CT images. In: WSCG'2021 - 29. International Conference in Central Europe on Computer Graphics, Visualization and Computer Vision'2021 (2021). https://doi.org/10.24132/CSRN.2021.3101.5

Automatic Forest Road Extraction from LiDAR Data Using Convolutional Neural Networks

Paul Georges, Phuc Ngo[✉], and Philippe Even

Université de Lorraine, CNRS, LORIA, 54000 Nancy, France
{hoai-diem-phuc.ngo,philippe.even}@loria.fr

Abstract. Accurate location of access roads is important for forest management, in particular in mountain areas. In this paper, we are interested in their detection from LiDAR data using deep learning approaches. For this, we use images computed from an interpolated surface, called *digital terrain model* (DTM), of the 3D point cloud. In order to train and validate the neural network models, two ground truth datasets associated to DTM images are considered: (1) manual digitization of the road centerlines and (2) automatic extraction followed by supervised completion using two softwares based on discrete geometry tools. The trained network models are then evaluated over a test dataset using standard measures such as precision, recall, F-measure and prediction time.

Keywords: Road detection · mountainous area · LiDAR images · CNN

1 Introduction

Forest road location and characterization are important information used for various purposes in forest management and such activities as wood harvesting. Their maintenance is also of great concern for planning team interventions on forest fires, in particular in mountain areas where accessibility may be quite difficult. In this context, airborne laser scanning, also called LiDAR (Light Detection And Ranging), is of great help to survey forested mountain areas. It is a 3D acquisition technique based on the emission of a laser beam swept over the measured scene and on the detection of reflected signal from the surface. In forested terrains, the received signal is composed of multiple echoes corresponding to the successive hit obstacles, from the forest canopy, down to lower vegetation levels and finally to the ground itself. From lower cloud points, classified as *ground points*, an interpolated surface, called *digital terrain model* (DTM), is computed using optimization techniques. An example of DTM image is given in *Fig.* 1 a.

Numerous studies have been proposed in the literature for road extraction from LiDAR data. Most of them deal with urban and peri-urban areas, for instance [1,12]. They are not well suited to rural context. Large standardized logging roads (see *Fig.* 1 b) are easily detected, but the sole topographic information is not sufficient to distinguish the pathway from bare earth borders at the

© The Author(s), under exclusive license to Springer Nature Switzerland AG 2023
B. Kerautret et al. (Eds.): RRPR 2022, LNCS 14068, pp. 91–107, 2023.
https://doi.org/10.1007/978-3-031-40773-4_8

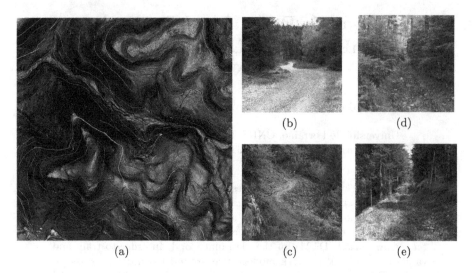

Fig. 1. (a) A shaded digital terrain model (DTM) image of size 4000×4000 pixels and $0.25\,\mathrm{m}^2$/pixel resolution, that corresponds to a $4\,\mathrm{km}^2$ area. (b–e) Different forest road types in mountainous context: (b) logging road with large vegetated shoulders at the same height, (c) shrinked road crossing natural screes, (d) eroded hollow road, and (e) unused road left to growing vegetation. (Color figure online)

same level, that are used for log stocking. They are generally well documented and not of major interest in our study. Smaller roads are more difficult to process as they show quite irregular surfaces and strong width variations along their layout. This may come from local terrain constraints (see *Fig.* 1 c), natural erosion (see *Fig.* 1 d), irregular maintenance or even complete relinquishment when they are not anymore used (see *Fig.* 1 e). Some attempts have been done to use the DTM to detect main roads on large-scale LiDAR [10,16,22,24]. Fewer works suggested to process raw data in complement to DTM analysis [1,2,12]. In particular, signal intensity was used to recognize road surface response. However, these approaches depend strongly on local terrain features, and parameters are difficult to set in practice. Raw altimetric information could also help to better discriminate roads, but its processing is generally considered as complicated.

Recently, a new framework, based on efficient discrete geometry and mathematical morphology tools, has been proposed in [8] for extracting automatically forest roads from LiDAR data. It is composed of two steps. First, the DTM image is analyzed to find relevant locations for detecting roads, then for each of these selected seeds, road sections are extracted using only raw LiDAR ground points. By processing ground points, the detection is more aware of the heterogeneous point distribution in the raw data. This helps to overcome the limits of DTM interpolation. The extraction framework was successfully tested on a large-scale LiDAR dataset. However, as mentioned in [8], it may not provide a good detection for complex road sections such as tight curves and intersections.

Convolutional neural networks (CNNs) based on deep learning technology are widely used in many different applications of image processing and analysis including semantic image segmentation. Due to their learning capabilities from training data, deep learning methods have performed remarkably well on many image analysis tasks and they lead to very successful results compared with traditional methods. Recently, they have been applied in road extraction from airborne LiDAR data [16,22]. In [22], a pixel-to-pixel architecture based on fully convolutional neural network is used to perform automatic mapping of small roads. This network provides good results for large-scale data. However, it may be bad at making local adaptions as mentioned by the authors. Higher performance could be achieved, but at the price of larger complexity and computational cost. In [16], a Dense Dilated Convolutions Merging Network (DDCM-Net) is proposed for multi-class segmentation of forest roads in the purpose of mapping road networks. The proposed architecture relies on multiple dilated convolutions merged with various dilation rates. It allows the network to learn more robust feature representation with densely linked dilated convolutions and to recognize effectively multi-scale and complex-shaped roads. In [17], this work was extended to a more general segmentation task using grouped convolutions and strided convolutions, in order to enhance the discrimination of small objects for a complete land cover classification task.

Inspired by the works [7,8,16], the current study aims at developing a fast, accurate and operationally simple deep-learning-based method, which considers information obtained from shaded DTM maps to detect the forest road in mountainous areas. More precisely, we use two softwares based on discrete geometry tools: ILSD (Interactive Linear Structure Detector) [7] and AMREL (Automatic Mountain Road Extraction from LiDAR data) [8] to generate the training dataset of forest roads from DTM images and LiDAR data. These data are fed to a convolutional neural network. In particular, we consider the binary branch of DDCM-Net [16] designed for a road segmentation task, and here adapted to the detection of narrow forest roads. Actually, it is quite difficult to segmentate these changing objects on a geometrical basis, in particular to provide reliable ground truths. The trained network models are then evaluated over a test dataset using the standard measure (precision, recall, F-measure). Another dataset, with manual annotations of forest roads represented by their centerline, is used to evaluate the improvement and the efficiency of the neural network in comparison to AMREL results [8] for forest road detection. The implementation of the neural network architecture, the trained models and execution procedure for road predictions are available at: https://github.com/paulgeorges1998/Light-DDCM-Net.

The rest of the paper is organized as follows: *Sec.* 2 describes our problem of forest road extraction and recalls the previous works related to this problem as well as the DDCM-Net architecture used in this work. *Sec.* 3 explains the experimental setup: dataset and network training, and *Sec.* 4 presents the experimental results. Finally, *Sec.* 5 gives a conclusion and draws some perspectives.

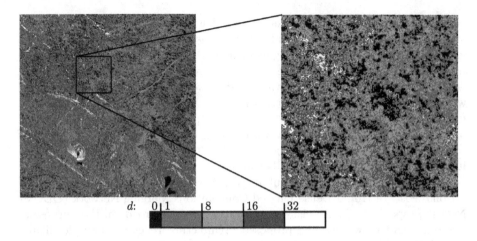

d: 0 1   8   16   32

Fig. 2. Detail of the ground point density map; the color corresponds to the number d of points per pixel ($1\,\mathrm{m}^2$).

2   Method

2.1   Problem Statement

The present work addresses the problem of automatic extraction of forest roads from the grayscale images of digital terrain model (DTM) associated to LiDAR ground point cloud. The DTM is encoded as a normal vector map obtained by derivation of the original height map. To visualize a DTM, hill-shading is a widespread technique based on controllable directional light sources. For detection purpose, we rather use slope-shading which can be seen as a lighting by a zenital source obtained by the normal vector z-component. As pointed out in [24], slope-shading ensures a good contrast between low gradient road surface and steep adjacent road cuts. In mountainous context, the interest objects – forest roads – correspond to *mostly flat zones* compared to the surroundings and this distinguishes them from the background. The slope-shaded DTM is a good representation allowing to enhance the flat zones. This is very beneficial for a learning process with neural networks to detect the forest roads.

Contrarily to road detection in urban and peri-urban areas using LiDAR data in which road characteristics are quite regular and well-contrasted, the case of forest roads is more challenging because of their wide range of shape and geometric features, and moreover, the large variations of the ground point density. Actually, dense vegetation impedes the laser beam from reaching the soil, and thus produces a heterogeneous distribution of the ground points as illustrated in *Fig.* 2. Such local lack of points makes the road detection task more difficult. Furthermore, sparse data may cause large approximations in the delivered DTM.

The purpose of the present study is to investigate the performance of a simple *deep-learning-based algorithm* combined with available LiDAR and image

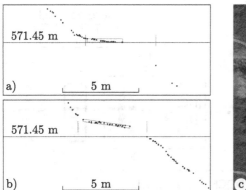
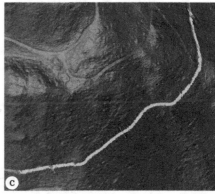

Fig. 3. A forest road extraction: a) altimetric profile collected at start scan (matched plateau enclosed, inaccurate right border location because of point lack); b) altimetric profile collected at scan 20 (tilted plateau); c) detected road over the DTM view (one scan on ten is displayed, manual seed in green, next scans in blue). (Color figure online)

processing tools to automatically detect forest roads in mountainous areas using shaded DTM images. More specifically, this problem can be seen as a binary segmentation with DTM images as input, and a binary image as output with white pixels indicating forest roads and black pixels for background, *i.e.*, not forest road. To that end, we selected a network architecture based on dilated convolutions at different rates [26]. Considering the complexity of goal objects, such convolutions will allow the network to have very large receptive fields and to learn scale-invariant features, and therefore recognize effectively multi-scale and complex-shaped roads with similar textures and intensities from input images.

2.2   Previous Approach to Forest Road Extraction

This work follows a former project on linear structure extraction, that resulted in two open-source softwares: ILSD [6] and AMREL [5].

ILSD allows the interactive extraction of linear structures, such as ridges, holloways or forest roads, from LiDAR raw data, *i.e.*, the set of 3D points classified as "ground" [4]. It relies on a scanline approach, where the user draws a stroke across a visible structure in the DTM view. Ground points lying in this manual seed are collected to get an altimetric profile, matched to a model of the structure cross profile (see *Fig.* 3 a). In the case of forest roads, the selected cross profile is approximated by a nearly horizontal plateau bounded by slope sides. This model fits well to mountainous context. In case of success, the structure is extended on both sides of the manual seed using adjacent scans and collected profiles (see *Fig.* 3 b). Spatial consistency is checked between successive altimetric profiles. All the processing is based on discrete geometry tools: blurred segments [3] or adaptive directional scans [9]. A several hundred meters long section can be extracted in a fraction of a second (see *Fig.* 3 c). Details of the extraction framework are provided in [7].

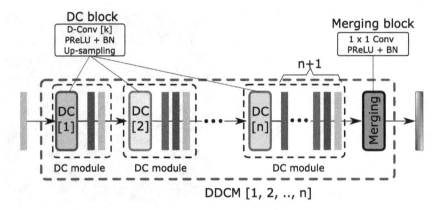

Fig. 4. A DDCM module is composed of n dilated convolution (DC) blocks of various dilation rates $k \in \{1, 2, \ldots, n\}$ and a merging block. Each DC block is composed of a dilated convolution (D-Conv) of rate k, followed by a parametric rectified linear unit (PReLU) activation, batch normalization (BN) and bilinear up-sampling. The output of DC block is then concatenated with its input together to feed the next layer. The merging block is composed of a 1×1 convolution (Conv) with PReLU and BN in order to efficiently combine all stacked features generated by intermediate DC blocks.

AMREL is focused on the automatic extraction of forest roads from LiDAR data [8]. Here, input seeds are automatically selected by processing slope-shaded views of the DTM. First a mathematical morphology operator, RORPO [19], is applied to enhance elongated shapes. Then straight edges are detected using FBSD [9], and seeds are arranged across the longest ones at regular intervals. Finally, each seed is processed by the scanline approach to obtain a collection of road sections. Performance evaluations showed a recall measure (ratio of correct detection area on whole detection area) of 70 ± 3 %, and a precision measure (ratio of correct detection area on ground truth area) of 81 ± 7 %. False detections most often occur at places with similar cross profiles to roads, for instance talwegs or cultivation terraces, and also in flat areas where the road section model is not well adapted. Undetected road sections correspond (i) to tight changes in direction where more seeds are needed to cope with the scanline approach directionality, (ii) to roads with large slope or irregular surface exceeding parameter thresholds, (iii) to areas with low point density.

Both tools can reliably be used to provide road ground truth maps. Their main drawback is the large amount of parameters to set. Most are directly connected to application needs, such as high or low bounds of road width, slope or tilt thresholds, ... But others take more time to set as they rather control internal details of the detection process.

2.3   Light DDCM-Net Architecture

In [16], a dense dilated convolutions merging network (DDCM-Net) and a joint-task learning structure with an iterative-random-weighting strategy for the joint-loss are proposed for a multi-class segmentation of forest roads from 2-band LiDAR images. In the proposed architecture, the DDCM-Net uses dilated convolutions [26] of stride 2 to learn features at varying dilation rates and merging by a concatenation of feature map at each layer with the feature maps from all previous layers. Such densely linked dilated convolutions and the fusion of feature maps is called a *DDCM module* and illustrated in *Fig.* 4. The DDCM modules allow the network to have very large receptive fields with just a few layers and to capture scale-invariant features of the detected objects.

The DDCM-Net architecture is composed of multiple DDCM modules with progressively increasing dilation rates to learn and to capture scale-invariant features of the detected objects. In [16], the DDCM-Net is integrated in a joint-task learning strategy, called an *end-to-end pipeline of the Joint-Task DDCM-Net*, to perform road segmentation and mapping tasks. In particular, the proposed architecture is composed of two parts: an encoder of low level features encodes multi-scale contextual information from the initial 2-band LiDAR images by a DDCM module with 6 different dilation rates (1, 2, 3, 5, 7, 9), and a decoder of high level features decodes highly abstract representations learned from the deep residual network (ResNet) pre-trained on ImageNet [21] by 2 DDCM modules, one with rates 1, 2, 3 and 4, the other with rate 1. The low-level and high-level feature maps by DDCMs are then fused together to infer pixel-wise full-class probabilities. The network outputs a multi-class segmentation which predicts what types of roads are in the input and a binary segmentation which locates all roads. More details of the Joint-Task DDCM-Net architecture are given in [16].

In this work, we are interested in the binary segmentation of forest road location from DTM images. For this purpose, we consider only the binary branch of the Joint-Task DDCM-Net in [16], called *L-DDCM-Net* (for Light DDCM-Net). The L-DDCM-Net architecture used in this work is illustrated in *Fig.* 5 in which we add a convolution of two 3×3 kernels and a concatenation with the input image, to create an image of 3 channels, followed by a batch normalization (BN) and a parametric rectified linear unit (PReLU) on top of the pre-trained ResNet [21]. In compatibility to Tensorflow, we remove the bilinear up-sampling in DDCM modules and use the dilated convolution of stride 1 with same padding instead without noticeable performance loss. For the loss function, we consider the standard binary cross entropy (BCE) loss [11]. More details about the training of L-DDCM-Net are given in *Sec.* 3.2.

3   Experimental Setup

3.1   Dataset

To our knowledge, no LiDAR test set of forest roads with ground truth is publicly available. This is certainly due to a large variability between different acquisition contexts and terrain configurations and maybe also to the huge data storage required. Many high resolution LiDAR campaigns are designed for archaeological prospections to reveal small topological details. In regards to sensitive aspects of cultural heritage material, access to this data is most often restricted. This

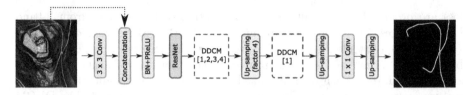

Fig. 5. L-DDCM-Net architecture used for our forest road extraction from LiDAR data. It is composed of a standard convolution, a concatenation with the input data followed by BN and PReLU on top of the ResNet50 pre-trained layer, a DDCM module with rates 1, 2, 3 and 4, a bilinear up-sampling of factor 4, an other DDCM module of rate 1, then a bilinear up-sampling, an 1×1 convolution and a final bilinear up-sampling.

is the case of the LiDAR acquisition used for this study [15]. Nevertheless, this set is large enough to test our L-DDCM-Net architecture. It covers the Fossard mountain area in upper Mosel valley in Eastern France, where four sectors of 4 km^2 each have been selected. Two of them include arranged areas for walking with a large variety of tracks (*Saint-Mont* and *Cuveaux*). The other ones (*Gris-Mouton* and *Grand-Rupt*) are mostly wood exploitation sectors, the last one featuring some large logging roads. Each DTM image resolution is 4000×4000 pixels (0.5 m pixel size). From these four sectors, two ground truth datasets associated to DTM images are considered:

- Set 1 is a **manual annotation** of each road centerline on the DTM. This set serves as a basis to compare with AMREL results.
- Set 2 is a **semi-automatic segmentation** using AMREL and ILSD sofwares. This set is used to train our network.

About the set 1, for each sector, most salient roads were carefully delineated in DTM views. Only the centerline was manually extracted. The achieved poly-lines constitute the road ground truth [8]. Due to the difficulty to characterize forest roads and to the long and tedious task of manual annotation, it is important to note that this ground truth is not perfect: several road portions have probably been omitted or wrongly annotated. Besides, the representation with centerlines does not provide us the width of a road.

For the set 2, we use the existing tools ILSD and AMREL to generate the forest road ground truth semi-automatically. It allows us to create the data in a simpler, faster and more efficient way. To that end, AMREL is first used to automatically extract road sections. The obtained map is then cleaned to remove obviously bad detections using some image processing tools. Finally, the ground truth map is completed in supervised mode using ILSD software. In particular, we can obtain the road width thanks to the detector of AMREL and ILSD. Contrarily to the set 1, the segmented roads in this dataset are *thick objects*. This enables the network to learn more discriminant features and receptive fields about the detected objects comparing to the centerline representation. Examples of data from both datasets are given in *Fig.* 6.

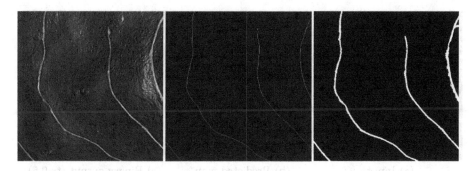

Fig. 6. Sample from training data. Left: shaded DTM image. Middle: Ground truth from set 1 of manual segmentation with centerlines of roads. Right: Ground truth from set 2 of semi-automatic segmentation of forest roads using AMREL and ILSD.

3.2   Network Training

We implemented the L-DDCM-Net described in *Sec.* 2.3 in Python using Tensorflow [23] and Keras [14] libraries which allow to parallelize and optimize many operations via the use of GPU.

For each sector, the DTM image and its corresponding ground truth are split into patches of 256 × 256 pixels without overlap in order to avoid correlation in both training and validation data during the training process. After the splitting process, we obtain 1024 patches in total, about 256 for each sector. Then, data augmentation operations are applied to the resulting patches to enlarge further the data: random rotation with angle in range 0° to 360°, horizontal flip with probability 0.5. Note that this data augmentation is applied only on the training images and performed *on the fly*, *i.e.*, during the training process.

We perform a k-fold cross-validation, with $k = 4$, to estimate the performance of the L-DDCM-Net on the available data. It consists in training k models by varying the data used for training and testing in such way that the model is tested once on k different folds. In other words, a sector is evaluated on a model trained with the other three sectors. Four models are trained on groups of patches with a ratio of 80% to the training set and 20% to the validation set.

The whole training process was done on GPU (NVIDIA GeForce RTX 3060 Laptop GPU graphics card with 16Go RAM). We used the Adam optimization algorithm with weight decay (AdamW) [18] with the two parameters $\beta_1 = 0.9$ and $\beta_2 = 0.990$ (default values in Tensorflow), and set the weight decay at 0.00005 and the learning rate at 0.00012.

We trained our network for 80 epochs, each epoch being comprised of 76 steps with 8 images per batch. Several values have been tested, and we come out with those values for the smallest BCE loss function on the validation. It should be mentioned that our training is quite fast. It takes about 15 min the whole process, and the interference time is about 5 s for each 4 km²-wide sector.

From the predicted probability maps, a threshold of 0.5 is applied to retrieve a binary image in which the white pixels correspond to forest roads and black

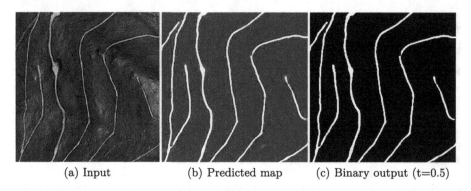

| (a) Input | (b) Predicted map | (c) Binary output (t=0.5) |

Fig. 7. Example of output of the trained L-DDCM-Net on a part of Gris-Mouton sector.

otherwise. This hyper-parameter can be let to user control according to task requirements, as it sets a balance between detecting as many roads as possible and reducing the rate of false detections. We can see in *Fig.* 7 an example of output of the trained network.

4   Results and Discussions

This section shows the experimental results of L-DCMM-Net for forest road segmentation. Experiments are divided into two parts. Firstly, we compare the performance of L-DCMM-Net with other CNN architectures: U-Net [20] and convolutional block attention module (CBAM) [25] on the data of set 2. Secondly, we evaluate the improving performance of L-DDCM-Net to forest road extraction in comparison with the previous work of AMREL on the manual data of set 1.

U-Net [20] is a fully convolutional network. It is originally designed for bio-medical image segmentation, and widely used in other fields. This architecture is well-known for its performance when trained with very few images which is the case of our forest road extraction.

Recently, in many CNN architectures, attention mechanism is usually added in order to make CNNs learn and focus more on important information, rather than learning non-useful background information. Among the different attention modules, convolutional block attention module (CBAM) [25] is well-known for its performance, light-weight and general module. It can be integrated into any CNN architecture seamlessly with negligible overhead and is end-to-end trainable along with the CNN. In order to check whether CBAM modules could help to improve the segmentation results of forest road extraction, they are combined with L-DDCM-Net in two different ways.

- L-DDCM+3-CBAM: a CBAM module is placed at the convolution output of the ResNet block and of both DDCM blocks,
- L-DDCM+8-CBAM: five other CBAM modules are added at the level of each DC module (four for the first DDCM block, one for the second block).

Table 1. Comparison of different CNN architectures on data of set 2.

Sector	Method	Time (s)	R (%)	P (%)	F (%)
Saint-Mont	U-Net	7.28	79.40	81.56	80.47
	L-DDCM-Net	**5.13**	78.47	82.04	80.21
	L-DDCM-Net + 3-CBAM	5.52	**80.98**	79.99	**80.48**
	L-DDCM-Net + 8-CBAM	5.89	75.87	**82.97**	79.26
Gris-Mouton	U-Net	7.49	76.82	**98.33**	86.25
	L-DDCM-Net	**4.86**	**79.74**	95.37	**86.85**
	L-DDCM-Net + 3-CBAM	5.29	77.19	97.69	86.24
	L-DDCM-Net + 8-CBAM	5.79	77.18	97.55	86.18
Grand-Rupt	U-Net	7.30	76.32	87.89	81.70
	L-DDCM-Net	**4.83**	**78.87**	88.77	**83.53**
	L-DDCM-Net + 3-CBAM	5.26	73.61	91.56	81.61
	L-DDCM-Net + 8-CBAM	5.71	72.05	**92.20**	80.89
Cuveaux	U-Net	7.50	84.58	86.50	85.53
	L-DDCM-Net	**5.08**	83.73	89.00	86.28
	L-DDCM-Net + 3-CBAM	5.45	82.91	**89.39**	86.03
	L-DDCM-Net + 8-CBAM	5.65	**86.01**	87.55	**86.77**

To evaluate the different architectures, we consider the same evaluation metrics as in [8]: recall R, precision P, F-measure F as the harmonic mean of R and P. These metrics are given in *Eq.* 1.

$$R = \frac{\overline{D \cap G_L}}{\overline{G_L}}, \quad P = \frac{\overline{D \cap G_W}}{\overline{D}}, \quad F = \frac{2 * R * P}{R + P} \quad (1)$$

with D the set of pixels predicted as forest roads, G_W the set of pixels corresponding to a 20 pixels dilation of ground truth data in set 2, G_L the set of pixels corresponding to the centerlines of G_W obtained by Zhang-Suen skeletonization algorithm [27]. The dilated set G_W is assumed to enclose the real road set and to take into account possible inaccuracy in the detection method.

Tab. 1 summarizes the performance measures of the different architectures on the four test sectors for cross validation. Overall the experiments, L-DDCM-Net gives the fastest inference time. On average, it is about 33% faster than U-Net. This is consistent to the lower complexity of L-DDCM-Net (10.4×10^6 trainable parameters) compared to U-Net (18.9×10^6). Adding CBAM blocks to L-DDCM-Net slightly increases the inference time and the model complexity (12.5×10^6 trainable parameters). Note that the training time is divided by 3 with L-DDCM-Net ($\simeq 15$ min) compared to U-Net or L-DDCM-Net with CBAM blocks ($\simeq 45$ min).

Regarding the evaluation measures, U-Net and L-DDCM-Net show similar results, with small variations depending on the test area. There is not a clear

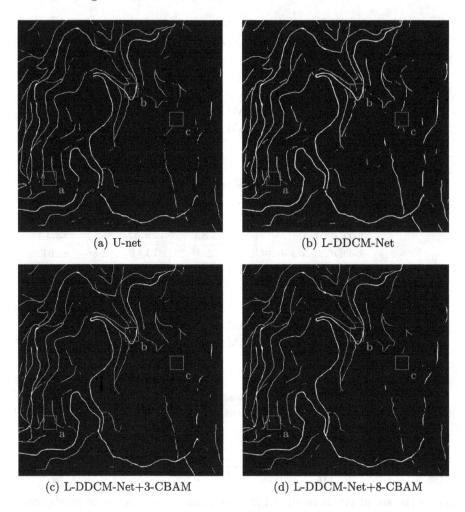

(a) U-net

(b) L-DDCM-Net

(c) L-DDCM-Net+3-CBAM

(d) L-DDCM-Net+8-CBAM

Fig. 8. Binary predicted maps obtained by different network architectures on Gris-Mouton sector. The networks are trained and tested with data from set 2. Hard configuration examples of *Fig.* 9 are located in green. (Color figure online)

difference when adding CBAM blocks to L-DDCM-Net. On wood exploitation sectors, Gris-Mouton and Grand-Rupt, achieved higher precision is balanced with recall decrease. But this observation does not hold anymore on the two other sectors, where both tested architectures for CBAM show contradictory results. However, better tuning for hyper-parameters could possibly be found to draw more benefits from attention modules for this task of forest road detection.

Figure 8 gives an example of prediction maps. We can observe that these maps, produced by the trained models, give a plausible forest road network. Some false positives match well visible road-like objects, that were not selected as ground truth because considered as short isolated sections or impracticable

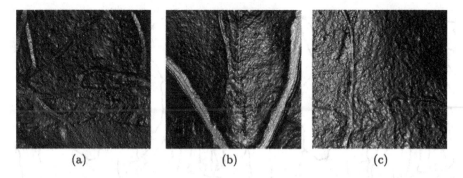

(a)   (b)   (c)

Fig. 9. Hard configurations for the detection task: a) DTM interpolations due to point lack, b) steep section at road junction, c) undisclosed road in flat area.

Table 2. Comparison between AMREL [8] and L-DDCM-Net using data in set 1 of manual road annotation with centerlines for the evaluation.

Sector	Method	R (%)	P (%)	F (%)
Saint-Mont	AMREL	67.46	74.90	70.99
	L-DDCM-Net	**76.72**	**79.01**	**77.85**
Gris-Mouton	AMREL	69.87	88.13	77.94
	L-DDCM-Net	**77.46**	**91.74**	**84.00**
Grand-Rupt	AMREL	73.01	78.37	75.60
	L-DDCM-Net	**78.44**	**86.94**	**82.47**
Cuveaux	AMREL	68.73	80.49	74.14
	L-DDCM-Net	**80.61**	**87.32**	**83.83**

roads. Many undetected parts are connected to blurred areas in the DTM image possibly due to a lack of ground points (see *Fig.* 9 a). Others correspond to narrow steep or damaged roads left back to erosion or vegetation (see *Fig.* 9 b). Moreover, roads crossing flat areas at almost the same height are undisclosed in this low contrasted part of the slope-shaded map (see *Fig.* 9 c). Already hard to delimit during manual digitization, such objects have few chance to be retrieved successfully by the network.

It must be noted that the measured performance values should be taken with caution. Many processes during the training of a deep network model are based on random selections, so that this step is certainly not reproducible. For each tested configuration, only the best model obtained on a small series of trials was kept. Therefore, we mostly conclude that among the 4 network architectures evaluated, L-DDCM-Net provides faster inference speed while maintaining high accuracy in detection. Hereafter, we use L-DDCM-Net as reference model for the next experiments.

To evaluate the improvement and the efficiency of the L-DDCM-Net for forest road extraction, we compare the results of the trained models with those of

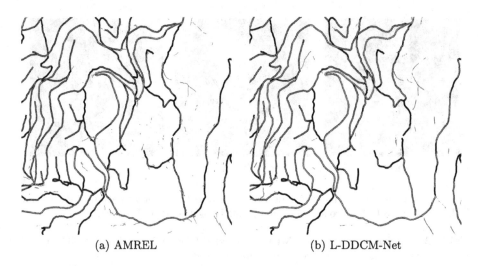

(a) AMREL	(b) L-DDCM-Net

Fig. 10. Comparison between AMREL (a) and L-DDCM-Net (b) using the ground truth data from set 1. Precision maps: dilated ground truth in black, good detection in green, false detection in red. (Color figure online)

AMREL on the data in set 1. For this, we consider the same evaluation metrics as in previous experiments (see *Eq.* 1). In particular, the set G_L is the centerlines of data in set 1 and G_W corresponds to a 28 pixels dilation of G_L. The comparison of both methods is reported in *Tab.* 2. L-DDCM-Net outperforms AMREL. L-DDCM-Net presents, on average, a performance increase of 8.5% in recall and 5.8% in precision on the four sectors. It takes 5 s to process a sector using L-DDCM-Net. Although it is not possible to compare this execution time with the 30 s reported for AMREL in [7] run on slower hardware, up to now, it is not guaranteed that this last could be adapted to GPU programming.

Figure 10 illustrates the results on one of the sectors. We observe less discontinuities and false detection in L-DDCM-Net results than in AMREL. This makes the results more favorable and complete in this task of forest road detection.

All implementation of L-DDCM-Net and execution procedure to reproduce the test results of Gris-Mouton sector in *Tab.* 1 and 2 are available at:

https://github.com/paulgeorges1998/Light-DDCM-Net.

Because other sectors cross well-known archaeological areas, it is unfortunately not possible to let a full access to the whole data set. For the test of the three other sectors and the training on all sectors, access to relevant DTM tiles may be requested to the LiDAR data owner.

5   Conclusion

This paper addresses the forest road detection in LiDAR data using deep learning approaches. More precisely, we consider digital terrain model (DTM) images computed from an interpolated surface of the 3D LiDAR point cloud. Two datasets, one from manual annotation with centerline and the other from a semi-automatic extraction using two softwares AMREL and IDSL, are used for training, validating and testing the method. Different convolution neural networks (CNNs) are considered in this work: L-DDCM-Net, U-Net and CBAM attention blocks. The trained network models are also compared with the AMREL results to show the improvement and the efficiency of the deep learning approaches for the problem of forest road detection.

In general, the CNNs provide high detection accuracy in addition to a fast prediction time. However, they also have several limitations in the present case. Firstly, we do not observe significant improvements by modifying the different architectures: adding attention modules, modifying the hyper-parameters, ... This may be due to the restricted amount of data used for training the CNN. In order to improve the CNN performance, we may need to provide more meaningful information to the network. Observing the false negative results, undetected forest roads often correspond to narrow steep sections, that are less contrasted in slope images. For traffic convenience, most of forest roads do not deviate significantly from isolines. In order to guide the networks to learn such behavior, we suggest providing not only the slope intensity, but also its direction as additional training data. The slope direction can be computed from the triangulated mesh used to build the DTM, and represented as a second input image. Furthermore, bigger size of training images could be considered to better capture the global context of the forest roads. Next availability of more general purpose LiDAR data at country-wide scale [13] will hopefully facilitate a complete reproducibility of this kind of work, including training stages. Combined with digitization facilities brought by AMREL and ILSD softwares, it will contribute to the production of such a wider training dataset.

Acknowledgements. DTM images are derived from Fossard LiDAR data acquired in scope of the PCR AGER project (*Projet collectif de recherche "Archéologie et GEoarchéologie du premier Remiremont et de ses abords"*), dir. Charles Kraemer, HIS-CANT Laboratory, Université de Lorraine.

References

1. Clode, S., Rottensteiner, F., Kootsookos, P., Zelnicker, E.: Detection and vectorization of roads from lidar data. Photogramm. Eng. Remote Sens. **73**(5), 517–536 (2007). https://doi.org/10.14358/PERS.73.5.517
2. David, N., Mallet, C., Pons, T., Chauve, A., Bretar, F.: Pathway detection and geometrical description from ALS data in forested montaneous areas. Int. Archives Photogramm., Remote Sens. Spatial Inform. Sci. **38**(part 3/W8), 242–247 (2009)
3. Debled-Rennesson, I., Feschet, F., Rouyer-Degli, J.: Optimal blurred segments decomposition of noisy shapes in linear time. Comput. Graph. **30**(1), 30–36 (2006). https://doi.org/10.1016/j.cag.2005.10.007

4. Even, P., Grzesznik, A., Gebhardt, A., Chenal, T., Even, P., Ngo, P.: Interactive extraction of linear structures from LiDAR raw data for archaeomorphological structure prospection. Int. Archives Photogramm., Remote Sensing Spatial Inform. Sci. XLIII-B2-2021, pp. 153–161 (2021). https://doi.org/10.5194/isprs-archives-XLIII-B2-2021-153-2021

5. Even, P., Ngo, P.: AMREL: Automatic mountain road extraction from LiDAR data. https://github.com/evenp/AMREL.git/ (2022)

6. Even, P., Ngo, P.: ILSD: Interactive linear structure detector. https://github.com/evenp/ILSD.git/ (2022)

7. Even, P., Ngo, P.: Live extraction of curvilinear structures from LiDAR raw data. ISPRS Ann. Photogramm. Remote Sensing Spatial Inform. Sci. **2** 211–219 (2020). https://doi.org/10.5194/isprs-annals-V-2-2020-211-2020

8. Even, P., Ngo, P.: Automatic forest road extraction from lidar data of mountainous areas. In: First Joint Conference on Discrete Geometry and Mathematical Morphology, pp. 93–106 (2021). https://doi.org/10.1007/978-3-030-76657-3_6

9. Even, P., Ngo, P., Kerautret, B.: Thick line segment detection with fast directional tracking. In: Proceedings of 20th International Conference on Image Analysis and Processing, pp. 159–170 (2019). https://doi.org/10.1007/978-3-030-30645-8_15

10. Ferraz, A., Mallet, C., Chehata, N.: Large-scale road detection in forested mountainous areas using airborne topographic lidar data. ISPSR J. Photogramm. Remote Sensing **112**, 23–36 (2016). https://doi.org/10.1016/j.isprsjprs.2015.12.002

11. Goodfellow, I., Bengio, Y., Courville, A.: Deep Learning. MIT Press (2016)

12. Hui, Z., Hu, Y., Jin, S., Yevenyo, Y.Z.: Road centerline extraction from airborne LiDAR point cloud based on hierarchical fusion and optimization. ISPRS J. Photogramm. Remote. Sens. **118**, 22–36 (2016). https://doi.org/10.1016/j.isprsjprs.2016.04.003

13. IGN: LIDAR HD - Une cartographie 3D du sol et du sursol de la France. https://geoservices.ign.fr/lidarhd/ (2022)

14. Keras: Python interface for artificial neural networks. https://keras.io/ (2022)

15. Kraemer, C., et al.: ArchéoGÉographie du premier Remiremont et de ses abords : le Saint-Mont et le massif du Fossard. Rapport de Projet AGER 1, Université de Lorraine (2018)

16. Liu, Q., Kampffmeyer, M., Jenssen, R., Salberg, A.B.: Road mapping in LiDAR images using a joint-task dense dilated convolutions merging network. In: IEEE International Geoscience and Remote Sensing Symposium, pp. 5041–5044 (2019). https://doi.org/10.1109/IGARSS.2019.8900082

17. Liu, Q., Kampffmeyer, M., Jenssen, R., Salberg, A.B.: Dense dilated convolutions' merging network for land cover classification. IEEE Trans. Geosci. Remote Sens. **58**(9), 6309–6320 (2020). https://doi.org/10.1109/TGRS.2020.2976658

18. Loshchilov, I., Hutter, F.: Decoupled weight decay regularization. In: 7th International Conference on Learning Representations (2019). https://doi.org/10.48550/arXiv.1711.05101

19. Merveille, O., Naegel, B., Talbot, H., Najman, L., Passat, N.: 2D filtering of curvilinear structures by ranking the orientation responses of path operators (RORPO). Image Processing On Line **7**, 246–261 (2017). https://doi.org/10.5201/ipol.2017.207

20. Ronneberger, O., Fischer, P., Brox, T.: U-net: Convolutional networks for biomedical image segmentation. In: 18th International Conference on Medical Image Computing and Computer-Assisted Interventions, pp. 234–241 (10 2015). https://doi.org/10.1007/978-3-319-24574-4_28

21. Russakovsky, O., et al.: ImageNet large scale visual recognition challenge. Int. J. Comput. Vision **115**(3), 211–252 (2015). https://doi.org/10.1007/s11263-015-0816-y

22. Salberg, A.B., Trier, Ø.D., Kampffmeyer, M.: Large-scale mapping of small roads in lidar images using deep convolutional neural networks. In: Scandinavian Conference on Image Analysis, pp. 193–204 (2017). https://doi.org/10.1007/978-3-319-59129-2_17

23. TensorFlow: Software library for machine learning and artificial intelligence. https://www.tensorflow.org/ (2022)

24. White, R.A., Dietterick, B.C., Mastin, T., Strohman, R.: Forest roads mapped using LiDAR in steep forested terrain. Remote Sensing **2**(4), 1120–1141 (2010). https://doi.org/10.3390/rs2041120

25. Woo, S., Park, J., Lee, J.Y., Kweon, I.S.: CBAM: Convolutional block attention module. In: Proceedings of the European Conference on Computer Vision, pp. 3–19 (2018). https://doi.org/10.1007/978-3-030-01234-2_1

26. Yu, F., Koltun, V.: Multi-scale context aggregation by dilated convolutions. In: International Conference on Learning Representations (2016). https://doi.org/10.48550/arXiv.1511.07122

27. Zhang, T.Y., Suen, C.Y.: A fast parallel algorithm for thinning digital patterns. Commun. ACM **27**(3), 236–239 (1984). https://doi.org/10.1145/357994.358023

Discussions Report Paper

Promoting Reproducibility of Research Results in International Events (Report from the 4th RRPR)

B. Kerautret[1]([⊠]), K. Kirchheim[2], D. Lopresti[3], P. Ngo[4], and P. Tomaszewska[5]

[1] Univ Lyon, Univ Lyon 2, CNRS, INSA Lyon, UCBL, LIRIS, UMR5205,
69676 Bron, France
bertrand.kerautret@univ-lyon2.fr
[2] Otto-von-Guericke-University, Magdeburg, Germany
konstantin.kirchheim@ovgu.de
[3] Lehigh University, Bethlehem, PA 18015, USA
lopresti@cse.lehigh.edu
[4] Université de Lorraine, LORIA, UMR 7503, Villers-lès-Nancy, France
hoai-diem-phuc.ngo@loria.fr
[5] Warsaw University of Technology, Faculty of Mathematics and Information Science,
Warsaw, Poland
paulina.tomaszewska3.dokt@pw.edu.pl

Abstract. Following the fourth edition of the workshop on Reproducible Research in Pattern Recognition (RRPR) at the International Conference on Pattern Recognition (ICPR), this paper reports the main discussions that were held during and after the workshop. In particular, the integration of reproducible research inside an international conference was the first main axis of reflection. Further discussions addressed the ways of initiating or imposing reproducible research, as well as the problem of performance comparisons of published research papers that emerges due to the fact that the reported results are often based on different implementations and datasets.

1 Introduction

Open science practices, such as sharing data and code, are important in computer science for advancing the field as a whole and, in particular, the reproducibility axis. They can help to increase the transparency and reproducibility of research. Encouraging researchers to adopt these practices can increase the impact and credibility of their research. Relying on the advances of new platforms supporting reproducible research [1], in this paper we explore some solutions to the challenges of improving reproducibility in computer science.

Following the RRPR workshop, two main axis were defined in order to guide the discussions on reproducible research (RR). The first point considered the methods to promote and incentivize RR at international conferences (Sect. 2). This part includes new proposals on how to address the topic of RR followed by some reflections on potential effects and impact measures of the current solutions. The second axis was more oriented toward motivating RR on platforms

© The Author(s), under exclusive license to Springer Nature Switzerland AG 2023
B. Kerautret et al. (Eds.): RRPR 2022, LNCS 14068, pp. 111–123, 2023.
https://doi.org/10.1007/978-3-031-40773-4_9

like *CodeOcean* and on the key reproducibility issues in computer science communities (Sect. 3).

In the rest of the paper, the reproducibility term will refer to the definition given by the Association for Computing Machinery (ACM) [2] which is the capacity to obtain results by a *"person or team other than the authors, using, in part, artifacts provided by the authors"*. From the same reference, replicability refers to results obtained by *"a person or team other than the authors, without the use of author-supplied artifacts"*.

2   Addressing RR at International Conferences

A starting point for the discussion on this topic was to analyze how reproducible research is currently being addressed at some international conferences in the computer science field. This was inspired by the study of Raff [3] who analysed over 255 papers in machine learning, and reported that only 63.5% could be replicated successfully (or reproduced, under the ACM definition [2]). In the following, we review different proposals that have been made to integrate RR in international conferences and events.

2.1   Recent Proposals

NeurIPS Checklist for RR. We started the analysis by identifying current practices addressing the topic of RR using the example of one of the largest international conferences in Artificial Intelligence – Neural Information Processing Systems (NeurIPS). In the case of NeurIPS, authors are asked to attach a *Paper Checklist* [4] during submission.

This requirement is an outcome of the NeurIPS 2019 Reproducibility program where a *Machine Learning Reproducibility Checklist* [5] was proposed (the revised version is available in [6]). This checklist covers various aspects that affect the reproducibility of the results, *e.g.,* model and algorithm descriptions (including complexity analysis), and the theoretical claims (including proofs) when applicable. It is also recommended to make the dataset publicly available together with its description and share details on the design choices made during training (like hyperparameters chosen, number of runs or dataset used).

In addition to the information on the checklist, it could prove beneficial to disclose the total training time, since resource requirements can drastically limit the number of individuals or institutions that can reproduce experiments (and there are also attendant environmental concerns due to the energy usage and carbon emissions) [7]. Moreover, information about the required dependencies to run the code should be provided, as well as information about the pretrained models (preferably including trained model weights).

Following an author feedback survey reported in [5], the NeurIPS general chairs proposed a simple checklist designed to help authors in assessing their research from the reproducibility standpoint by analyzing aspects defined in the *Machine Learning Reproducibility Checklist.* The authors are asked to fill out the checklist by answering *yes*, *no*, or *n/a*. Note that selecting an option other than *yes* does not necessarily entail the rejection of the paper. The checklist should rather initiate self-reflection. Moreover, it helps to identify the limitations of the contribution.

Other Methods of Checking the Requirements of RR. Conferences such as Artificial Intelligence and Statistics (AISTATS) or the European Conference on Computer Vision (ECCV) use a different approach to promote reproducibility of research. During submission, the authors are asked whether they will release the code and the datasets used in the paper. If they agree, the editors check whether the code/dataset are provided with the camera-ready version; for example, as an attachment, or in the form of a link to a public repository. If authors who previously agreed do not publish the code/dataset at the camera-ready stage, the article will not be accepted for publication. This policy imposes control over promises that are not kept by authors.

However, this verification may be rather limited because it is questionable whether the quality of the check is sufficient, since verifying the mere existence of source code/dataset does not guarantee the reproducibility of the results reported in the paper. Furthermore, since the code repositories remain under the control of the authors, they can be altered or removed after publication of the paper. However, still, this initiative should be considered positive, since it incentivizes authors to make the source code publicly available.

Another initiative is the Machine Learning Reproducibility Challenge which consists of an annual call over five successive years for reproducibility reports on papers published at eleven top Machine Learning conferences (including for instance NeurIPS, ICML or CVPR) or top journals [8]. Based on the RR definitions mentioned in the introduction [2], other approaches give incentives for authors to prioritize RR by offering awards or recognition for papers that are checked to be reproducible or replicable [9].

2.2 New Ideas on Promoting RR at International Conferences

To address the limitations of simple checks by editorial teams on whether a code/dataset was publicly shared, the discussion group would like to highlight the idea of introducing a special submission channel oriented to reproducible research. Here, the key principle is to ask authors interested in participating to complement their research submission with a technical description. Such a document should provide details on how the results from the submitted paper can be reproduced. More precisely, it should contain information on the requirements, dependencies, installation procedure, sets of parameters and instructions on how to run the code to reproduce the results described in the main paper. In exchange for the effort to provide such a document, the idea is to construct for authors an online demonstration that could be used to test the proposed model behaviour on a broader spectrum of use cases – not only on the ones presented in the main paper. In the discussion group, we analyzed the schedule for organizing such a special channel. We believe that it could be undertaken as follows:

1. **Preliminary call for Technical Reproduction Instructions Document (TRID).** At this first stage, a document should be uploaded before the deadline of the main conference paper (*e.g.,* one month before). It contains the key instructions on how to run the code of the proposed method/study. The provided instructions can help reviewers test the reproducibility of the research results. Moreover, they can also be considered a starting point for the construction of an online demonstration to be described next. Since the TRID is only a simple document containing technical instructions, it could be submitted before the main paper deadline, even if the algorithms in the paper might be modified later.

2. **Online demonstration and RR report.** In the second step, starting just after the TRID deadline, while the authors are finalising their main paper, the RR reviewing channel team will construct an online demonstration based on the submitted TRID. Future readers of the paper will benefit from such a demonstration which allows testing the method on various inputs without any installation or time-consuming processes. As described in the next point, the online demonstration could be also potentially passed on to reviewers.

   Note that the online demonstration construction could be realized by Master's students with Computer Science backgrounds who will be members of the RR reviewing channel team. For this, one could imagine that the conference chairs would cooperate with various university partners that are identified by the organizers before the event. Ideally, this identification would take place when a team applies to organize the conference. To manage the technical aspects of creating the demonstration, an online demonstration construction system can be used [10]. When an idea proves successful, we can also think about the deployment of the open-source demonstration system [11] in other infrastructures. For this task, the main point of attention should be a hosting system that ensures continuity over time and is accessible to future editions of the conference. Obviously, contributions by Master's students to the process should be recognized, *e.g.,* via a certificate where the details of the contribution are listed. In cases where constructing an online demonstration are too difficult or complex, a simpler alternative could be to require a simple report of code reproduction (RR report).

3. **Open access to reviewer board.** With a deadline that is one month earlier, the demonstration could be passed on to reviewers during the middle of the main paper reviewing phase. The online demonstrations or RR report would first be made available to the authors. After the authors have reviewed the prepared files, we could ask for permission to share them with the reviewers. Thanks to the earlier TRID submission deadline, it would be possible for authors to mention in the paper the limits of the proposed method that were identified using the demonstration.

An overview of this proposal is depicted in Fig. 1. The idea could be beneficial to students, researchers and reviewers. Thanks to the referencing system, each student who participates in the demonstation/RR report preparation process could receive proof of their research experience and will have demonstrated skills

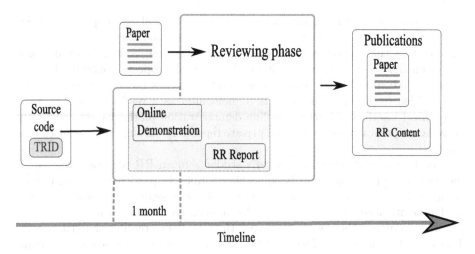

Fig. 1. Example of the proposed procedure to encourage the incorporation of the RR idea in conferences.

and interest in the topic. In addition, students will become familiar with the demonstration system and are likely to be more inclined to incorporate it into their future research. For authors, they would receive a proof of reproduction by another (hopefully objective) team which can be considered by reviewers in making their acceptance decisions. In particular, it will be more difficult for authors to miss limits of their method that they may not have noticed before. Finally, this can also be beneficial to reviewers, since they can now focus on the content of the paper instead of trying to reproduce the supplementary material.

Some questions can be asked about the potential impact of the required submission effort on the authors' willingness to submit their work to conferences that have such a requirement. To motivate them, the procedure for the RR submission should be as simple as possible for authors; such as, for the step of TRID, only a simple description would be required. This could be a formatted document similar to the content found in a Readme file on a project repository indicating the steps needed to install and run the code.

It may well be that the authors could potentially be more interested in devoting their time to work on another publication rather than to care about reproducibility issues. This could be linked to the "publish or perish" paradigm where there is pressure to publish as much as possible, as quickly as possible. In contrast, there is a slow science movement where more time is allocated to research and trying ideas that are innovative, and therefore with higher risk of failure. As a result, the papers are less frequently written. In the slow science movement, there will be more time to work on one topic and develop demonstrations. However, an approach like this that may reduce the number of papers and the number of conferences may be unpopular with conference organizers.

In most cases, building an online demonstration will not require a special effort on the part of authors who have already written their own code. It is possible that the authors will not want to publicize their code because it is not "clean enough" to be shared or due to intellectual property concerns. In such cases, the advantage of an online demonstration is that the source code can be kept hidden from the public if it is implemented as a ready-to-use API with a graphical interface. Moreover, online demonstration platforms are constantly evolving and now can be based on a private repository through the use of *Docker* images[1].

The idea of including the Master's students in an RR processes related to the conference is not necessarily something simple. In particular the organizing team needs to coordinate with supervisors of the Master's programs to ensure student motivation and availability. An alternative solution would be to ask people submitting their work to invest their time in creating the RR report. This way, the additional effort would be shared by everyone which would create incentives to make reproducibility as easy as possible.

2.3 Impact of Efforts Encouraging RR in Conferences

When analyzing examples of conferences that encourage RR and ways to evaluate its impact, a number of questions come to mind. Such information could help strengthen the appeal of RR to other international events. In particular, we raise the following questions:

(a) Have these steps been successful in either increasing the visibility of RR and/or the confidence of those who later cite the published papers that they are reproducible? This evaluation may require defining a new measure, as the number of citations by itself does not necessarily correlate with reproducibility. One could also consider download metrics of source code and data, or the success rate of reproducing research, *etc.*

(b) Are authors, reviewers and conference organizers generally satisfied with the processes? In other words, do they consider the required effort worth it? Feedback on the reproducibility process from authors and reviewers (*e.g.,* the ease of sharing data and code, the usefulness of the reproducibility materials, and the impact of reproducibility on their research, *etc.*) are important for improving the quality of RR and increasing its impact. Some partial answers can be found in the NeurIPS 2019 Reproducibility program report [5].

(c) It is important to note that some conferences are in high demand and have very low acceptance rates which means that they can require authors to do just about anything in the hopes of getting published. But holding such power over authors is a double-edged sword. If the new requirements make it harder to get the work published, who benefits from the new rules and who is hurt by them? It is probably too simplistic to say "good researchers benefit and bad researchers are hurt". Less selective conferences will find it difficult

---

[1] https://hub.docker.com/.

to request similar amounts of added effort from authors who may become even more likely to try for higher-rated conferences given the time investment required. The proposal described in Sect. 2.2 based on the TRID submission could be a way to attract authors who are curiosity-driven rather than those whose only aim is to publish. In the former case, researchers are interested in broadening awareness of their work, so reproducibility is important to them. In the latter case, researchers would mainly base their decision where to submit based on the acceptance rate of the conference.

(d) It is natural to ask whether any conferences have studied the aforementioned questions and reported the results. Making such an analysis seems to be imperative if changing the way a conference works is motivated by the idea of "improving" it. In the report of the NeurIPS event [5], it is stated that the perception of usefulness of the reproducibility checklist was analysed from the reviewers' point of view. However, it turned out that 34% of the reviewers find the checklist useful while the others either do not read it or find it not useful. Another interesting point is the fact that reviewers who find the reproducibility checklist useful tend to give better reviewing scores and better acceptance rates. The authors of the study also mention that the number of submissions continues to increase (from 40% between 2019 and 2020)[2] which suggests that the checklist does not impact the perception of the conference and the reviewing process negatively. Moreover, the number of authors willing to submit their code increased from 50% to 75%. Other questions remain open from the point of view of authors, but the existing study reports no negative consequence of incorporating the idea of a checklist into the submission process, which may encourage further steps in promoting RR at conferences.

Publishing the analysis and examining the impact of reproducibility requirements, as in the previous example, are good steps forward and should be encouraged across all conferences that have added requirements to ensure research reproducibility. Beyond this, further investigation and questioning are needed about the criteria that will help us understand whether these efforts are successful and whether the extra work by authors and reviewers is justifiable. Here we list some points that should be considered when evaluating the investment of time and the impact on the community through emphasizing RR in international events:

- How do RR practices affect the speed and efficiency of research in computer science?
- Does RR allow higher quality research papers because more time can be devoted to the parts of the paper that advance its new ideas?
- What are the potential benefits to authors for investing in RR? How would such data be captured and reported?
- How to properly measure and report about the failure rate when reproducing previous results?

---

[2] Source: https://github.com/lixin4ever/Conference-Acceptance-Rate (accessed on 2 April 2023).

- Is RR beneficial to graduate students? RR may allow graduate students to progress faster in their work and to produce stronger PhD dissertations because they will not have to spend as much time reimplementing past work. But, on the other hand, if reproducibility is "easier", they may lose an important learning opportunity for better understanding the work of others.
- Will we see faster progress toward major goals in the field? This would have to be defined and may not be easy to estimate. For example, we might ask whether there are fewer papers claiming small improvements on the state of the art, and more papers claiming significant improvements.

3   Focus on Motivating RR

Following the previous analysis of existing and new strategies for including RR in scientific events, the discussion here considers the motivations behind the use of the platforms facilitating RR and related issues.

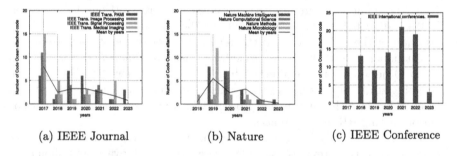

(a) IEEE Journal   (b) Nature   (c) IEEE Conference

Fig. 2. Evolution of *Code Ocean* attachments to papers published in *IEEE* reference journals (a), four *Nature* journals (b) and *IEEE* international conferences (c).([3]Extracted using filters in code ocean platform https://codeocean.com/explore?page=1&filter=withArticle in 26 March 2023.)

3.1   Recent Initiatives

Incentive or Obligation in RR. One point to consider relates to the choice between two approaches – motivation vs. obligation – for including a description of the RR measures undertaken in the published research. The previous example of the RR checklist at NeurIPS is an intermediate state. It asks for answers to the questions in the checklist, but lets authors state that some measures do not apply in their case and does not directly imply rejection of the paper. As mentioned in the previous section, authors and reviewers have found the use of a checklist to be a positive, and the number of submissions seems not to be negatively impacted.

Including RR Platforms in Journal Publication. IEEE also encourages authors to follow RR practices through publicly sharing code and data to facilitate use by others and confirmation of reproducibility. IEEE offers the option of releasing code online using the *Code Ocean* platform launched in 2017 (see [1] for a review on reproducible research platforms). Figure 2 shows the evolution over time of *Code Ocean* attachments mentioned. The number of code submissions to this platform appears stable or decreasing both in the case of *IEEE* and *Nature* journals (Figs. 2a and 2b). It remains relatively low in some cases; for instance, for *IEEE PAMI*, the highest rate of papers containing a *Code Ocean* demonstration was reached in 2019 at only 4.1% (considering 12 issues, each of them containing an average of 14 papers). On the other hand, the number of code capsules associated with publications in international IEEE conferences increased by over 68% from the period 2017–2019 to 2020–2022. Even if the aforementioned trend can be explained by other factors (like specific information campaigns, better knowledge of the *Code Ocean* platform), this suggests that authors are more and more willing to provide demonstrations of their work in international conference publications. This point can be an argument to justify the implementation of the scheme proposed in the previous section to encourage the inclusion of demonstrations in the publication pipeline.

Calls for Demonstration at Conferences. Initiatives like the Call for Demonstrations of IJCAI events appears to be a new way of encouraging RR with links between theory and practice [12]. This call gives authors the opportunity to publish a showcase of research results.

3.2 Issues for Research Result Comparisons

When a new method is proposed, its performance and properties are usually compared with current state-of-the-art methods from the field. Sometimes, this requires reimplementing previous methods as the code was not provided by the original authors. Such additional work is not really considered during the submission and review process. However, it could be of interest to the community. In such cases, maybe the replication could be considered to have value in itself and be recognised by a specific label indicating a post-hoc contribution to already-published work by publicly sharing the code for the replication. Such efforts, if encouraged, would likely require less of a time investment than proposing full-scale replication to a journal like ReScience [13] or IPOL [14].

Training Data. A lack of access to the data for which the results were reported makes reproducibility very difficult. Sometimes, authors cannot release data due to privacy and licensing concerns. This most often occurs when medical or health data is involved in the research, or data is confidential due to company policy (legal issues). In these cases the following solutions are possible:

1. In the paper, the performance of the proposed method could be reported not only on the private data but also on public date so that at least a part of the results can be reproduced. The possible drawback of this solution is that there might not be public data of a similar type, and using other data with a significant distribution shift would require employing a different method than the one being proposed.

2. In cases where it is not possible to share data, *e.g.,* due to legal issues, and there is no similar public data, the authors could give limited access to the private data to a specific certified, third-party entity that would be responsible for checking whether the results can be reproduced. To the best of our knowledge, there is currently no such well-established entity that can certify reproducibility (something similar to the Reproducible Label at the RRPR workshop). Such a certified entity would have to sign Non-Disclosure Agreements (NDA) to ensure that the confidential data will be used in a clearly defined way (whatever is necessary to perform the task) without sharing it with third parties. This idea follows the notion of cybersecurity testing by Red Teams, a service is often outsourced. This policy is more complex than the first one, and would only have to be considered if the first option does not apply.

3. In some cases, a hybrid solution may work, *e.g.,* when medical datasets cannot be fully publicly available. Researchers who would like to use the data must apply for access and sign an agreement specifying Terms of Use (sometimes there is also a requirement to be affiliated with a university). In some cases, the procedure is more complex and the applicant has to additionally complete an online course regarding the Terms of Use. This procedure is applied in the case of the MIMIC dataset [15].

Trained Model. Another way to improve the reproducibility of research is to not only provide the source code, but also the weights and other parameters of the trained models. Such models can then serve as foundation models [16] to facilitate further research of those who would like to build on the original work. Transfer learning is a related notion that is climate-friendly, as it decreases the number of computations during the model training, and therefore reduces carbon emissions which can be substantial for large models [7].

Processing data in such a way could be risky since it may be possible to infer private information. This could also happen due to model inversion attacks [17] that can potentially recover the training data. More recently, some entities have refused to publish model weights, noting ethical and safety concerns [18,19].[3]

3.3   Strengthening Reproducibility: From Publications to Teaching

Open to Coupled Publications. There is no doubt that reproducibility requires extra work on the part of authors and reviewers. In a world where

---

[3] However, for GPT-4 [19], OpenAI published the evaluation code, which makes comparison with their claimed results easy.

researchers aim to maximize the number of their publications, the extra effort required to follow RR best practices could be a barrier. A possible solution would be to provide additional publication opportunities so that authors receive more recognition depending on the additional work that they do. For instance, in addition to the main conference paper, the authors might be invited to submit another paper providing reproducibility details.

This paradigm would allow work corresponding to a single paper to get publication credit as two papers under a new model: a scientific paper and a paper focusing on its reproducibility. The two separate papers would both be submitted and reviewed at the same time, and if both are accepted, the authors would get two publications – double credit – to account for the extra work they have done. Such an approach is comparable to the "companion paper" initiative we proposed to the authors of accepted ICPR 2022 papers (and also repeated later for the ACM ICMR Reproducibility Track [9]). Such a solution would require some organizational adjustments to account for the extra work done by reviewers and conference chairs. The approach that has already been adopted in some cases is to increase the size of the program committee to match the additional work, perhaps dividing the responsibilities between reviewers who have the expertise to handle scientific submissions versus reproducibility submissions.

To avoid possible confusion, this new paradigm would also require a clear explanation in the Call for Papers so that authors understand the role played by the reproducibility companion paper and how both parts of the submission will be reviewed.

Reproducing Scientific Results and Teaching. Today, even though common licenses such as GPL and BSD require it, it is common for authors to provide their code without instructions on how to run it, or to omit key details (*e.g.,* running parameters, hardware or software configurations, *etc.*). Sometimes, the code is not provided at all. This can make the reproduction task difficult or even impossible.

In many scientific papers, it is often necessary to reproduce the results of other work (*e.g.,* when comparing the performance of different methods, or applying an existing method to a new problem area, *etc.*). While it can be an excellent educational experience to involve students, including them in an attempt to reproduce past work could raise the following issue. In the case that the reproduction attempt fails, it may be hard to distinguish the degree to which the failure is caused by the lack of reproducibility of the paper, or the competence of the *reproducer*. To address this point, an incentive structure can be created that motivates the reproducing party to put serious effort into the reproduction attempt. To implement this, a possible strategy could be to encourage multiple groups (that do not know each other) to independently reproduce the results. In the end, analyzing whether the majority of groups succeeded in their attempts could provide a broader picture of the reproducibility of a paper compared to a single yes-no answer. Groups whose reproducibility assessments fail to agree with the majority could potentially receive a negative score (in an educational scenario). This incentives students to put effort into the reproduction, since they must assume that others they are competing against will do the same. This straightforward approach for incorporating this idea into teaching could be a starting point for discussions leading to a more sophisticated approach. If all of the groups fail to reproduce the results, it may mean that the code (if provided) is not sufficiently complete, or that the paper is poorly written, at least from the standpoint of reproducibility. The latter reason may be due to the complexity of a particular topic where a high level of in-depth expertise is required to understand the publications. It may also be the result of tight page limits for the paper and any supplementary materials, which does not now allow sufficient space to fully describe the method. If none of the groups succeeds in reproducing the results, it could be interesting to study how this kind of information spreads throughout the research community. We assume that this situation already arises in practice, but that it does not receive enough attention.

Note that there will be work that cannot be reproduced with contemporary means by others since it would require too much computing power, time, money and expertise – for example, large language models like ChatGPT [20], or foundation models more generally. Here, the question arises of how to verify the reproducibility of these very recent solutions. We believe this class of extreme models will require the development of new methodologies.

4   Conclusion

Resulting from the discussion sessions organized during and after the RRPR workshop, this report addresses various questions on the integration of reproducible research in international events, and on motivating authors to apply RR good practices. Perspectives we discussed include the creation of new RR submission channels providing ways of integrating RR in the future. From the analysis of other recent initiatives designed to encourage RR, we anticipate growing degrees of success of these and other proposals to promote reproducible research in upcoming events in our community.

References

1. Colom, M., Kerautret, B., Krähenbühl, A.: An Overview of Platforms for Reproducible Research and Augmented Publications. In: Kerautret, B., Colom, M., Lopresti, D., Monasse, P., Talbot, H. (eds.) RRPR 2018. LNCS, vol. 11455, pp. 25–39. Springer, Cham (2019). https://doi.org/10.1007/978-3-030-23987-9_2
2. Artifact review and badging, 2020. Revised August 24. https://www.acm.org/publications/policies/artifact-review-and-badging-current. Accessed October 14
3. Raff, E.: A step toward quantifying independently reproducible machine learning research. In: Advances in Neural Information Processing Systems. Curran Associates Inc, (2019)
4. NeurIPS 2022 Paper Checklist Guidelines. https://neurips.cc/Conferences/2022/PaperInformation/PaperChecklist (accessed in 26 February 2023)

5. Pineau, J.: Improving Reproducibility in Machine Learning Research (a Report from the NeurIPS 2019 Reproducibility Program). J. Mach. Learn. Res., **22**(1) (2022). Publisher: JMLR.org
6. The Machine Learning Reproducibility Checklist. https://www.cs.mcgill.ca/jpineau/ReproducibilityChecklist.pdf. Accessed 13 Mar 2023
7. Strubell, E., Ganesh, A., McCallum, A.: Energy and policy considerations for deep learning in NLP. In: Proceedings of the 57th Annual Meeting of the Association for Computational Linguistics, pp. 3645–3650 (2019)
8. ML Reproducibility Challenge 2022, 2022. https://paperswithcode.com/rc2022,. Accessed 4 Mar 2023
9. ICMR reproducibility, 2023. https://icmr-reproducibility.github.io/website/cfp2023/, Accessed 4 Mar 2023
10. Arévalo, M., Escobar, C., Monasse, P., Monzón, N., Colom, M.: The IPOL Demo System: A Scalable Architecture of Microservices for Reproducible Research. In: Kerautret, B., Colom, M., Monasse, P. (eds.) RRPR 2016. LNCS, vol. 10214, pp. 3–16. Springer, Cham (2017). https://doi.org/10.1007/978-3-319-56414-2_1
11. IPOL demo system development. https://github.com/ipol-journal/ipolDevel. Accessed 26 Feb 2023
12. Call for demonstrations of the IJCAI international conference. https://github.com/ipol-journal/ipolDevelhttps://ijcai-23.org/call-for-demos. Accessed 1 Apr 2023
13. Rougier, N.P., Hinsen, K.: ReScience C: A Journal for Reproducible Replications in Computational Science. In: Kerautret, B., Colom, M., Lopresti, D., Monasse, P., Talbot, H. (eds.) RRPR 2018. LNCS, vol. 11455, pp. 150–156. Springer, Cham (2019). https://doi.org/10.1007/978-3-030-23987-9_14
14. Colom, M., Kerautret, B., Limare, N., Monasse, P., and Jean-Michel Morel. IPOL: a new journal for fully reproducible research; analysis of four years development. In: Badra, M., Boukerche, A.,mUrien, P., eds 7th International Conference on New Technologies, Mobility and Security, NTMS 2015, Paris, France, July 27–29, 2015, pp. 1–5. IEEE (2015)
15. Johnson, A., Bulgarelli, L.: Tom Pollard. Leo Anthony Celi, and Roger Mark. MIMIC-IV, Steven Horng (2021)
16. Bommasani, R., et al.: On the opportunities and risks of foundation models. arXiv preprint arXiv:2108.07258 (2021)
17. Fredrikson, M., Jha, S., Ristenpart, T.: Model inversion attacks that exploit confidence information and basic countermeasures. In: Proceedings of the 22nd ACM SIGSAC Conference on Computer and Communications Security, CCS '15, pp. 1322–1333, New York, NY, USA (2015). Association for Computing Machinery
18. Brown, T., et al.: Language models are few-shot learners. Adv. Neural Inf. Process. Syst. **33**, 1877–1901 (2020)
19. OpenAI. GPT-4 Technical Report. arXiv preprint arXiv:2303.08774 (2023)
20. van Dis, E.A.M., Bollen, J., Zuidema, W., van Rooij, R., Bockting, C.L.: ChatGPT: five priorities for research. Nature **614**(7947), 224–226 (2023)

Author Index

B. Kerautret et al. (Eds.): RRPR 2022, LNCS 14068, p. 125, 2023.
https://doi.org/10.1007/978-3-031-40773-4